Energy Update

Energy Update
Oil in the Late Twentieth Century

Michael Tanzer
and Stephen Zorn

Monthly Review Press
New York

Library of Congress Cataloging in Publication Data
Tanzer, Michael
  Energy update.

  Includes bibliographical references and index.
  1. Petroleum industry and trade. 2. Petroleum
industry and trade—Political aspects. 3. International
economic relations. 4. World politics—1975–1985.
I. Zorn, Stephen. II. Title.
HD9560.5.T349 1985   333.8'232'09049   84-27342
ISBN 0-85345-663-1
ISBN 0-85345-664-X (pbk.)

Monthly Review Press
155 West 23rd Street, New York, N.Y. 10011

Manufactured in the United States of America

10 9 8 7 6 5 4 3 2 1

To my beloved sons,
Charles, David, and Kenneth
—Michael Tanzer

For Jean with love
—Stephen Zorn

Contents

Introduction

Ten years ago one of us published a book entitled *The Energy Crisis: World Struggle for Power and Wealth*. Following closely on the historic 1973 Organization of Petroleum Exporting Countries (OPEC) price revolution, it focused on two key questions of that time. First, is there a real energy crisis in the sense of an oil shortage? Second, would the projected pile-up of petrodollars in the OPEC countries sink the world economy? On the first question, the conclusion was that "there is no real energy crisis, in the sense of a physical shortage of energy resources; rather, there is an artificially contrived scarcity generated by various forces operating within the overall framework of the international capitalist economy." On the second, it was speculated that "at this juncture it would appear that ultimately the most likely 'solutions' to the international oil problem would be either intervention by the developed countries in the Middle East, including possible use of armed force, to drive down the price of oil, or an international depression which by reducing sharply the demand for oil would help offset the impact of the recent oil price increases." Of the two, a world depression seemed the "more likely outcome."

The past decade, in our opinion, has essentially validated these conclusions. At the same time, new problems have come to the fore. The most visible is the replacement of supply crises and gas lines by demand crises and underutilized oil facilities. In addition, the OPEC financial surpluses have peaked and in some cases turned to deficits. All in all, the once front-page oil and energy story has been pushed to the back pages.

To downplay the importance of the oil sector now, however, would be as shortsighted and misleading as it was fifteen years ago, when even oil economists projected into the future the past decade of continually expanding oil production matched by continually falling crude oil prices—which by 1969 had fallen to $1.25 per barrel. Indeed the error would be even graver today, since the size of the industry in financial terms has increased by an order of magnitude to where it is now more than ever the largest and most crucial sector of the world economy.

The Key Players

The aim of the present book is exactly what its title states: to update our previous analyses to deal with the many crucial changes that have taken place in the last decade, and to try to see where these events are leading in the future. Toward these ends, we have used the same topical/historical approach as in the earlier work. This is because the key players in the energy world are still the same as those of ten (or thirty) years ago: the international oil companies and their home governments, the international financial institutions, the oil-importing industrial and third-world countries, the oil-exporting countries, and—crossing a number of categories—the centrally planned economies. And, since the century-long history of this key industry is still vital to understanding its present, we have included in abbreviated form some of the earlier history presented in The Energy Crisis, while focusing on events of the past decade.

One striking underlying theme emerges from both The Energy Crisis and the present volume; namely, developments in the international oil and energy industries are integrally linked, in both cause and effect, to the international capitalist system. To the extent that this system penetrated virtually everywhere in the post-World War II period and bound up its players in a tighter and tighter network of linkages, the smaller was the chance for any players to break out of the system. On the other hand, to the extent that the international capitalist system is now increasingly enmeshed in what in our view will be a prolonged economic crisis of stagnation, lasting probably through the rest of the twentieth century, the greater is the chance that some players may be able to break loose from historic roles.

Overall then, we conclude that the stability of the international oil industry, as a leading force in the international capitalist system, has reflected and will continue to reflect the degree of stability or crisis in the world economy. Put in historical perspective, the events of recent years validate once again the old notion that the more things change, the more they remain the same. Cataclysmic changes in the world system, however, will not leave the industry the same at all. To demonstrate how we arrive at this conclusion, we have to make a careful analysis of the major players in the international oil and energy industry. For this, a good picture of the supply/demand for energy resources is essential background.

1

Fueling the International Economy: Supply and Demand of Energy Resources

For most of the post-World War II period, the story of the international energy industry has been the story of oil. Even today, despite tenfold increases in the price of oil since 1973 and fevered efforts by the industrialized nations to develop alternatives to petroleum, oil and gas account for nearly two-thirds of the nonsocialist world's energy supply, and for 70 percent of U.S. energy needs. Only in China, Eastern Europe, and Australia do coal and other energy sources supply more than half of domestic requirements. And even the most optimistic predictions for such renewable energy sources as the sun, the wind, alcohol from sugarcane, or hydropower do not suggest that these will account for more than 8 to 10 percent of the world's energy before the year 2000. At least for the remainder of this century, energy issues will be largely petroleum issues.

Oil has not always been the dominant source of power. The petroleum age began, in fact, only a little more than a century ago, when Edwin Drake discovered oil in Pennsylvania in 1859. And until the end of the nineteenth century, the uses of petroleum were limited to the refining of kerosene for home heating and lighting and to lubricants. Around 1900, however, oil began to play a more prominent role. Fuel oil was used more widely in ships' boilers and industrial plants, while kerosene's importance faded. More important, the birth of the automobile age, which can be dated from the introduction of Henry Ford's Model T in 1908, made oil an indispensable fuel. By 1929 petroleum accounted for roughly one-third of U.S. energy consumption. The Great Depression of the 1930s slowed the rise of oil, however, and on the eve of World War II, oil and natural gas together still provided only 45 percent of total U.S. energy consumption. But during and after the war military, transportation, and industrial demand for petrofuels skyrocketed; by 1952, oil and gas provided two-thirds of U.S. energy, a proportion that has been more or less constant to the present.

The rest of the industrialized world, which did not experience the automobile boom of the United States, lagged behind in oil consumption. By 1950, for example, oil and gas provided only one-seventh of energy needs in Western Europe and one-fifth of those needs in the Far East. However, oil and gas use in these areas grew rapidly in the 1950s and 1960s, as fuel oil replaced coal for industrial use and an automobile industry began to spark the sort of fuel use that had earlier transformed the U.S. energy industry. By 1970, on the eve of the Organization of Petroleum Exporting Countries' (OPEC) oil price increases, petrofuels made up two-thirds of energy consumption in Western Europe and Japan as well as in the United States.

Planned Economies

The centrally planned economies—the Soviet Union, China, and Eastern Europe—have moved much more slowly in shifting from coal to oil and gas. In 1950 these countries relied on petroleum for the same proportion of energy needs as did Western Europe—one-seventh of total consumption. But by 1970 their dependence on oil and gas had risen only to 40 percent of total energy needs, as compared with two-thirds in the capitalist countries. Since then, oil and gas use in the Soviet Union itself has increased to the point where these fuels, produced from domestic reserves, now account for roughly the same proportion of total energy consumption as in the United States, Japan, and Western Europe. But in Eastern Europe and China, oil and gas were still, in 1982, the source of less than 40 percent of total energy consumption. This slower growth of dependence on oil is even more industry, where production decreased by more than 50 percent from 1955 to 1975, or to the loss of internal energy self-sufficiency or balance of payments considerations.

The process of replacing indigenous coal with imported oil was helped by the ability of the oil companies, using their low-cost reserves in the Middle East and Venezuela, to set a price for fuel oil that was so low that European and Japanese industrial consumers would prefer fuel oil to coal. The companies' pricing strategy was also based on their traditional emphasis on maximizing production and profits for gasoline sales in the U.S. automobile market, for which there was no alternative to oil. Thus if sufficient profits could be earned from gasoline sales, virtually any amount at all earned from the sale of other refined products, such as fuel oil, simply represented an additional bonus to the companies. Given low prices for fuel oil, and the need of West European and Japanese companies to compete in world markets with U.S. companies that were already using the same low-cost fuel oil, European and Japanese governments could not easily have adopted policies to keep out imported energy, even if they had not been subject to U.S. political and economic pressure.

Even in the United States, which had been virtually self-sufficient in energy, the advent of new low-cost crude, controlled by the oil companies, produced growing reliance on imported fuels. Oil imports averaged more than 3 million barrels per day, roughly one-third of total oil consumption, by 1970, and by 1977 imports had doubled to 6 million barrels per day, nearly 40 percent of total consumption.

Thus virtually all the leading industrialized capitalist countries, with the temporary exception (while North Sea supplies last) of Great Britain and the partial exception of the United States, as well as most of the developing countries have become overwhelmingly dependent on foreign crude oil for their energy supplies. And even the United States remains significantly linked to international sources of oil. Despite a decade of conservation and slower economic growth in the wake of the 1973 oil embargo and OPEC price increases, the Organization for Economic Cooperation and Development (OECD), the twenty-four-nation grouping of the industrialized capitalist countries of North America, Western Europe, and Japan, consumed more than twice as much oil as it produced in 1982.

Availability of Resources

Despite this dependence, there is no lack of available energy sources in most countries. The world as a whole is not "running out of energy." But there is a difference between energy sources that may exist and be physically recoverable and those that are classified as "reserves" and form the basis of economic forecasts and projections. As noted earlier, proven reserves are generally defined as those resources that are located in already discovered deposits and can be produced at current prices, using currently available technology. Obviously, the concept of reserves is an elastic one, which depends partly on the state of technology, which will affect the cost of production, and partly on the price of oil (or any other natural resource), which may be set by the market, by the companies, by OPEC, or by some combination of these forces. If new technology, for example, suddenly makes it economical to recover oil from far offshore areas, in water more than 1,000 feet deep, then the world's oil reserves will miraculously increase, with absolutely no new exploration effort. Similarly, if the price of oil rises to $100 a barrel or more—as some thought it would when planning for expensive synthetic fuel projects got underway in the 1970s—then billions of additional barrels of oil in such high-cost areas as the Canadian Arctic or small North Sea fields will immediately be added to proven reserves.

A further factor that limits the utility of published reserve figures is that much of the world has not been fully explored. As long as there is a sufficient quantity of a resource to meet foreseeable needs, there is very little incentive, especially for companies interested in short- and medium-term profits, to keep on exploring at a great rate. For example, there is undoubtedly far more oil in the Middle East than is reported in the published reserve figures. But once the international oil companies found hundreds of billions of barrels—more than they could expect to produce during the life of their concessions—they had little incentive to explore further within the region. Moreover, it is clearly in the interests of the oil companies, which still control a significant proportion of oil supplies in the nonsocialist countries, to paint a picture of scarcity so as to support efforts to keep prices high and government taxes and charges low. Despite wide fluctuations in the price of oil over the past twenty years, however, the ratio of reserves to current production has been remarkably stable, ranging from a low of twenty-seven years' production (in 1979, just before the second major OPEC price increase) to a high of thirty-five years' production in 1970, at the end of a long period of fixed, low prices.

In comparison with the economically and politically influenced figures for proven reserves, the available data on physically recoverable energy resources are far less pessimistic. In a recent review of energy studies, the congressional Office of Technology Assessment cited more than half a dozen scholarly estimates of ultimately recoverable world crude oil resources that agreed on a figure of from 1,600 to 2,300 billion barrels, or from 80 to 115 times current annual consumption levels. Similarly, the world's available natural gas is estimated at more than 150 times annual consumption, while recoverable coal deposits would provide supplies sufficient to meet current levels of consumption for 500 years. More expensive but technically feasible resources contain additional centuries of potential energy supplies. The world's largely unexploited oil shale deposits, for example, are believed to contain more than 200 times the amount of energy potential that is in conventional oil fields. And none of this calculation takes into account the vast possibilities of renewable and nonpolluting energy sources, such as the sun, wind, tides, waves, ocean temperature gradients, or geothermal energy—all of which may be preferable to the use of fossil fuels such as oil and coal—let alone to the enormously dangerous but theoretically possible vast expansion of nuclear power. (This discussion of potential energy sources ignores the undesirable economic and environmental impact of certain forms of energy, such as the problem of disposing of nuclear wastes, or the "greenhouse effect" on the earth's climate caused by the burning of hydrocarbons. These considerations may well lead to a decision to forgo certain energy sources.)

Distribution of Resources

It is true that the world's known energy resources tend to be distributed unequally relative to population. But despite the fact that three-fourths of the world's coal reserves, for example, are in the United States, the Soviet Union, and China, there are many other countries that have sufficient coal to cover their domestic energy needs for many years to come. India, for example, which uses oil for one-third of total energy needs, has indigenous coal reserves that would amount to 600 years' worth of current consumption. Even in oil-importing Western Europe, coal reserves could supply eighty times the annual energy consumption in West Germany and fifty times the energy consumption in Great Britain.

The basic data on current patterns of energy consumption and production and the location of likely major sources of energy for the years to come can be summarized briefly. (Detailed data are given in tabular form in the Appendix.)

As might be expected, global energy consumption is heavily concentrated in the industrialized countries, especially the United States. As Table 1.1 in the Appendix shows, the United States, with some 5 percent of the world's population, still uses more than a quarter of the world's energy. The OECD group of industrialized countries as a whole uses more than half the world's energy, while the Soviet Union, Eastern Europe, and China account for another one-third, leaving less than one-sixth of energy supplies for all developing countries together. The extent of these disparities in human terms is suggested by data on per capita energy consumption. In the United States in 1982, for example, each man, woman, and child used the equivalent of 49 barrels of oil. In the twenty-four-country OECD group, the figure was 29 barrels, while in the socialist countries energy consumption was 10.5 barrels per capita. In contrast, per capita energy use in the third world was only 2.4 barrels.

Oil and Gas

Oil and gas still account for the bulk of energy supplies, even after a decade of higher prices and conservation efforts. As Table 1.2 in the Appendix shows, the relatively small decline in total oil consumption has hit the OPEC countries very hard; their oil production has fallen precipitously since the early and mid-1970s, while production in most other countries has remained relatively stable or (as in the case of North Sea oil) increased.

The relatively low share of Middle Eastern countries in world oil production in the 1980s—barely one-fifth, as compared with their possession of more than half the world's known reserves—marks one of the fundamental changes in the world oil industry since the price and supply shocks of 1973. The OPEC countries in general, and the Middle East in particular, from the point of view of the industrialized nations have become suppliers of last resort, and are increasingly compelled to adjust their production rates to worldwide demand fluctuations. In addition, the OPEC countries' status as suppliers of last resort makes them vulnerable to manipulation of demand (for example, by building or running down inventories) by the oil companies and by the home governments of those companies, which can have major effects on the OPEC countries' economies.

Worldwide natural gas production, on the other hand, has increased fairly steadily in the last decade. Among the more significant recent developments are the emergence of a worldwide market (especially in Japan and to a lesser extent the United States) for liquified gas from developing countries (the main suppliers are Indonesia, Malaysia, Brunei and Algeria), and the increasing importance of the Soviet Union as an exporter of gas to Western Europe. This latter trend will continue through the 1980s with the completion of the Yamal gas pipeline linking Siberian fields with European markets. (Data on production and reserves of natural gas are shown in Table 1.3 in the Appendix.)

Coal

Recoverable reserves of *coal* are somewhat more evenly distributed. The United States, the Soviet Union, China, Great Britain, West Germany, India, South Africa, Poland, and Australia all have large, identified coal reserves. In addition, many countries, including a large number of developing countries, possess medium-sized coal deposits that could be significant in meeting their domestic or regional energy needs. (Data on coal production and reserves are shown in Table 1.4 in the Appendix.)

International trade in coal, in contrast to that in oil, is carried out almost exclusively among the industrialized countries. Any coal produced by developing countries is consumed domestically, for the most part. This pattern may change in the next decade, however, as additional developing countries begin importing coal for power generation, and as such coal producers as China enter the international market.

Hydroelectricity

The last major conventional energy source is *hydroelectric power*. Hydro potential is concentrated largely in the third world. Where large-scale uses for such power exist, as in the heavy-industry developments of Brazil and Argentina, or where investment in aluminum smelting or other energy-intensive industries has created a large demand, as in Ghana and Suriname, it has been possible to develop hydro potential on a large scale. Most of the world's potential remains undeveloped, however, because of the high per-unit capital costs and economies of scale that have made smaller plants uneconomical.

Solar Energy

For other potential sources of less conventional renewable energy, such as solar power, wind, waves, tides, or conversion of biomass, no worldwide inventory exists. Since the most promising source at this time appears to be *solar power*, we will briefly review its history and estimates of its future prospects.

Scientists have known for over a century that sunlight could be converted into electricity, but its practical development awaited the right combination of technological innovation and energy economics. As one writer has noted:

> The photovoltaic effect—that light falling on certain materials can cause a spark of electricity—was first recorded in 1839 by French physicist Edmund Becquerel. In the 1880s, costly selenium photovoltaic cells were constructed which had a one to two percent efficiency (the amount of sunlight on the cell which is actually converted to energy). In 1954, a Bell lab research team discovered that silicon (one of the most abundant and low-cost materials on earth)

possessed properties allowing a photovoltaic effect. The space program gave photovoltaics its next big boost when the National Aeronautics and Space Administration (NASA) used silicon solar cells on Vanguard I, the second U.S. satellite launched in the late '50s.

However, it was not until the 1970s when the OPEC price increases drove the cost of fossil fuels up sharply and increased concerns about the security of oil supplies that solar power really began to be taken seriously. In later chapters we will analyze the institutional forces that have brought solar power in the last decade to the verge of a dramatic take-off. Here it will suffice to point out that in the last ten years increasing research and development have greatly increased the efficiency of solar cells, from 8 percent to about 20 percent efficiency, with forecasts for continuing progress over the next ten years. In addition, as mass production begins, manufacturing costs per unit will decrease owing to economies of scale. Given this, most forecasts foresee a continuation through at least the rest of the century of the high growth rates in solar power already achieved in the last decade—on the order of 50 percent per year.

Nevertheless, given the tiny base from which solar power is starting, even at high growth rates it will take a long time to rival fossil fuels. For example, a recent (1984) admittedly conservative forecast of U.S. utility installation of photovoltaic cell generating capacity projected an average increase of 82 percent per year through the year 2000, which still left all solar power with far less than 1 percent of total electrical capacity. Moreover, for some uses—notably land, sea, and air transportation—there are no likely substitutes for petroleum in the rest of the twentieth century. Therefore it seems safe to assume that for this period at least, no matter how effectively new energy technologies are developed, petrofuels will continue to dominate world energy markets.

Exactly how and by whom new energy technologies (as well as old energy sources) are developed is itself, however, a function of the interplay of institutional forces in the international energy economy. As always, at the eye of this hurricane are the international oil companies, which have dominated the scene throughout the century. We thus turn to an examination of their role as the keystone to our energy update.

2

The Big Seven: The Rise of the International Oil Giants

Today's international oil companies represent the greatest concentration of private economic and political power in the history of modern capitalism. Yet, although it might seem that these companies have always been a part of the capitalist scene, in historical terms these giants are relative newcomers. The granddaddy of the big oil companies, John D. Rockefeller's Standard Oil (now Exxon), is little more than a century old, and most of the large companies it begat are much younger. For nearly a century, the history of these companies was a history of growth and ever-expanding influence. Only in the past decade have they been seriously challenged, primarily by the governments of the oil-producing countries. Despite these challenges, however, the companies' power and profits remain at levels unmatched by those of any other industry.

Harvey O'Connor, one of the first serious analysts of the international oil industry, wrote in 1955:

> For a half-century the history of oil was also the personal history of John D. Rockefeller, who tamed an anarchic industry and brought it under the direct control of Standard Oil. The oft-told tale ran the spectrum of the devices of monopoly. Competitors were bought out or ruined, legislators and public officials were also bought out . . . laws were flouted with impunity or by stealthy indirection.

Rockefeller made his first investment in oil in 1862, three years after Edwin Drake had completed the world's first commercial oil well. By 1870 Rockefeller had formed the Standard Oil Company, uniting several refineries in Cleveland, Ohio, then the center of oil-processing activity. For most of its early life, Standard OIl concentrated on building a monopoly in the refining and distribution fields, leaving the riskier work of oil exploration and production to small-scale entrepreneurs. In these early days, for the oil drillers, the promise of riches could easily turn to ruin. In 1860, a year after Drake's discovery, oil brought its producer $20 a barrel; by the end of the next year, as hundreds of new wells were brought into production, the price had collapsed to $.10 a barrel. Sometimes, a barrel of oil was actually cheaper than a barrel of water.

Rather than cope with these risks, Rockefeller focused on refining and transportation. He persuaded the railroads to give him rebates on his oil shipments, and persuaded other refiners to join with him or sell out, while the oil producers, weakened by overproduction and their own inability to combine effectively, were left with no alternative but to take the price Rockefeller offered. Standard Oil became virtually the only buyer for crude oil in the United States, and as the industry spread from Pennsylvania into Ohio, Kansas, and California, the Rockefeller monopoly spread with it. Near the end of the nineteenth century, Standard Oil had a virtual world monopoly over oil processing and distribution.

The Monopoly Under Pressure

This near monopoly was undermined by discoveries of large new fields around the world. In Europe in the late 1880s, the Nobel and Rothschild interests developed Russian and Rumanian oil into a major competitor to Standard Oil. At the same time, oil was discovered in the East Indies (now Indonesia) and the Bataafsee Company, the predecessor of Royal Dutch/Shell, was organized in 1890, competing with Standard for the proverbial unlimited market for "oil for the lamps of China." Despite these challenges, however, at the end of the nineteenth century Standard held two-thirds of the British market, four-fifths of the continental European market, all of Latin America, and three-fifths of Canadian markets, in addition to its dominant position in the United States.

More significantly, Standard's control in the United States began to weaken with the 1901 discovery of the Spindletop field in
Texas, the largest find up to that time in North America. Out of the
need for capital to develop and market this bonanza, the original
finders turned to Andrew Mellon, banker and industrialist, who
formed Gulf Oil Corporation to handle this transaction. The
Spindletop field also increased competition for Standard Oil
when the Texas Corporation (Texaco) obtained leases there and
Shell Transport and Trading Company of London undertook to
market some of the oil, largely to the British navy.

In 1911 Standard Oil was broken up by antitrust action of the
U.S. government, and the company was divided into a number of
large regional oil companies, of which the most important were
Standard Oil of New Jersey (now Exxon), Standard Oil of New
York (now Mobil), Standard Oil of California, Standard Oil of
Indiana, and Standard Oil of Ohio. The first three of these spin-off
companies, together with Gulf, Texaco, Royal Dutch/Shell, and
British Petroleum (the latter was originally established in 1908 as
the Anglo-Persian Oil Co. and in 1914 came under British government control) formed the seven majors, sometimes known as the
"seven sisters," which have dominated the international oil industry during the twentieth century.

Within the United States a dozen or so smaller oil companies
grew to considerable size after the break-up of Standard Oil, although their operations rarely reached outside the borders of their
home country. These companies included Atlantic Co. (now Atlantic Richfield), Tidewater Oil (now part of Texaco), Continental
Oil Co. (now owned by DuPont), Union Oil, Phillips, Sinclair
(now part of Atlantic Richfield), and Cities Service (recently acquired by Occidental). All these companies were primarily domestic operations, with little impact outside the United States,
although in the post–World War II boom years of the oil industry
many of them did venture into international exploration.

Battles Among Companies

Until 1928, the history of the international oil industry was a
continuous series of struggles for markets and profits, primarily

between Standard Oil of New Jersey and Royal Dutch/Shell. In the mid-1920s, Standard and Shell were fighting for access to Iraq's oil, for Soviet oil, and for markets in all corners of the world. The tactics used ranged from price wars and bribery to violence. As Standard Oil's official historian noted: "For its unsavoury reputation, the world petroleum industry could only blame its leaders, fighting with all the means at their command—the worse as well as the better—to channel the forces of militant nationalism and to restore an economic system which was not to be restored."

This international oil war ended with a formal peace agreement, negotiated in 1928 at Achnacarry Castle in Scotland by the heads of Standard Oil of New Jersey, Royal Dutch/Shell, and British Petroleum. Under this agreement, the three companies agreed to fix their market shares at the 1928 level and to eliminate price competition (by setting the price of low-cost Middle East oil equal to that of high-cost production from the Gulf of Mexico, thus guaranteeing super-profits on their Middle East production).

By the late 1940s, when the postwar economic boom promised expansion for the oil industry, all seven companies had become well established internationally. Standard Oil of California (Socal), which had not been a party to the 1928 agreement, had obtained concessions in Saudi Arabia in 1936, opening up the vast Saudi reserves. Socal joined with Texaco, which already had strong Eastern Hemisphere marketing operations, to form Aramco, the Arabian-American Oil Co., which became the world's largest single producer. (The story of how the Saudi oil concession was negotiated is told in more detail in Chapter 3.) Mobil acquired a 10 percent interest in Aramco in 1946, at the same time that Standard Oil of New Jersey took a 30 percent interest. Meanwhile, Gulf, which had most of its overseas production in Venezuela, moved into the Middle East in 1934 when in partnership with British Petroleum it obtained a concession in Kuwait.

By 1949 the seven majors accounted for almost three-fifths of the nonsocialist world's total crude oil production and refining capacity, and large shares of marketing and transport as well. Even these figures fail to give a true picture of the big companies' profitability; the seven companies provided only one-third of U.S. oil, which had high costs and relatively low profits, but almost nine-tenths of the low-cost, high-profit crude oil from Latin America and the Middle East. Thus the seven majors probably earned close to three-fourths of all oil industry profits in this period.

Among these companies, however, there were great differences in size. Standard Oil of New Jersey, by far the biggest company, produced one and one-half times as much crude oil as Royal Dutch/Shell, the next largest, and four times as much as Mobil. Even after more than two decades of very rapid growth, on the eve of the Organization of Petroleum Exporting Countries' (OPEC) price revolution in 1973 these relative rankings had changed very little. Exxon (formerly Standard of New Jersey) was still the leading company, producing more than three times as much crude oil as Mobil.

Changes in the 1970s

The massive changes in the international oil industry from 1973 onward, however, have altered the collective dominance of the seven major companies. By 1982, out of a total oil production in the world's market economies of some 38 million barrels per day, the seven majors accounted for only 16 million barrels, or roughly two-fifths, compared with over three-fifths a decade earlier (see Table 2.1 in the Appendix). Moreover, the 1982 figure for the companies' production includes not only oil that they own themselves, but also oil that they purchase under "buy-back" arrangements with Middle East and other OPEC state oil enterprises. At the same time, the relative ranking of the companies has shifted, with Royal Dutch/Shell replacing Exxon as the largest producer, and Gulf falling behind Mobil into seventh place.

The key to the long period of collective dominance by the seven majors prior to 1973 was the rapid growth of the third world in general and the Middle East in particular as a source of crude oil, along with the relative decline of the United States as a source of production. In 1949, when the world's total oil reserves were estimated at about 75 billion barrels, the United States was thought to have about 40 percent of that total, and the Middle East a similar share. Today, even though drilling has been a hundred times more intense in the United States than in the rest of the world, this country is thought to have only 5 percent of world oil reserves (which are now estimated at 600–700 billion barrels), while the Middle East's share is generally put at 50–60 percent. (This changing picture reflects both relatively wasteful drilling in the United States stimulated by favorable tax laws and the abundance of oil nature bestowed on the Middle East.) From 1949 to 1972, the Middle East's share of world oil production increased from 15 percent to 38 percent.

Control of high-profit crude oil production has also made big oil companies among the most significant concentrations of economic power in the capitalist world. As early as 1947 three of the seven companies—Exxon, Mobil, and Texaco—were among the ten largest U.S. industrial companies, measured in terms of assets. In 1983 five oil companies—the three just mentioned plus Standard of California and Standard of Indiana—were all in the top ten U.S. industrial firms. In terms of profits, even before the 1973 price increases, the five largest U.S. oil companies earned $3.8 billion, or roughly one-seventh of all the profits of the Fortune 500. By 1983 the same five oil companies accounted for $10.3 billion in profits, or slightly more than one-seventh of the Fortune 500's total (see Table 2.2 in the Appendix).

The vast post–World War II expansion of the oil industry allowed room for other oil companies to grow as well. While in 1947, sixteen of the one hundred largest industrial companies in the United States were oil companies, by 1972 that number had increased to twenty and by 1983 to twenty-four; moreover, in 1983, fifteen of the twenty-five largest U.S. industrial companies were oil firms.

In general, the growth of all these companies, both the seven majors and the so-called independents, involved a process of increasing "vertical integration"; this movement by most companies into all stages of the oil production process was dictated by the drive to minimize risk. Companies that found large quantities of crude oil integrated "forward" into refining and marketing in order to have outlets for this crude, particularly in times when there was a glut of crude; conversely, marketers and refiners found it necessary to integrate "backward" into crude oil production in order to have assured supplies, particularly at times when crude was scarce. Vertical integration became the rule in the industry, and today most all large U.S. oil companies operate at every level of the industry.

The expansion of the oil industry was also a process of geographical expansion, in search of the lowest-cost oil supplies and, especially since OPEC appeared to take control of the pricing process in the early 1970s, in search of politically "safe" places to look for oil. While the current strategies of most major companies focus on the United States and such "safe" areas as the North Sea, that was by no means always true. The importance of the third world in general and the Middle East in particular in fueling the growth of the oil companies cannot be overestimated.

Until World War II, despite the acquisition of some overseas concessions, most of the big U.S. oil companies were primarily domestic. Only Exxon, which drew two-thirds of its crude oil from outside the United States, could have been called a truly international company. By 1972, however, the situation had fundamentally changed. Exxon was then producing 80 percent of its oil overseas, and 40 percent from the Middle East alone. That same region accounted for two-thirds of Standard of California's production, three-fifths of Gulf's, and half of Texaco's and Mobil's. Even a formerly wholly domestic company such as Standard Oil of Indiana was producing two-fifths of its oil in the Middle East by the early 1970s.

The Majors' Share Declines

Since 1972 the big oil companies have begun to lose their stranglehold over world oil supplies, as producing countries have taken more direct control over local oil industries. There has also been a general trend in the established crude oil producing areas toward government ownership of production facilities. More than one hundred countries have established their own national oil companies, with mandates to participate in exploration, development, production, refining, and sale of petroleum, and most of the major producing countries have acquired either full or majority ownership of their oil operations. As a result, the ownership share of all the international oil companies in world crude oil production has decreased sharply from the level of a decade ago, from 94 percent in 1970 to 41 percent in 1981. The share of the seven major companies declined even more, from 61 percent in 1970 to 22 percent in 1981 (see Table 2.3 in the Appendix).

However, the big oil companies account for a larger share of the oil that is traded internationally than the above figures suggest. In many cases where governments nationalized crude oil production, the companies that formerly owned the oil fields retained the right, after nationalization, to purchase a large share of the crude oil from the country's state oil enterprise. In 1982, for example, of all the crude oil produced outside the socialist countries and North America, 43 percent was either produced by or purchased by the seven major companies.

As OPEC countries and other third world governments took over ownership of crude oil production, the companies increasingly lost their ability to ensure crude supplies to their own refineries. For the oil companies, in the face of these new developments, one strategy of the 1970s was diversification—into other resource industries and even into other industries, such as electrical machinery, retailing, or office equipment, that had nothing to do with oil or mineral resources.

Some diversification had already taken place in the 1950s and early 1960s, when most oil companies moved heavily into the petrochemical business. This was in a sense a natural extension, since the companies already produced natural gas, the basic raw material for most petrochemicals (chemicals derived from petrofuels rather than coal). In addition, the industrial processes in chemicals were similar to those in oil refining. Moreover, the companies had cash available to make the $100 million-plus investments required to build chemical plants. Thus by 1962 oil companies owned or operated over one-third of all U.S. petrochemical plants, and petrochemicals in turn accounted for more than three-fifths of the total output of the U.S. chemical industry.

Coal and Nuclear Power

In the next wave of expansion, beginning in the 1960s and gaining momentum in the 1970s, the oil companies began entering competitive energy industries, particularly coal and nuclear power. Their mixed success in petrochemicals, where their profits were much lower than in oil and gas production, reinforced the companies in their belief that their greatest advantage was as near-monopolistic suppliers of raw materials. As noted earlier, the enormous profits of the five U.S. majors, as well as those of the foreign majors, Royal Dutch/Shell and British Petroleum, in the 1950s had been based on their near-total control over low-cost crude oil from the Middle East and Venezuela. The expansion into coal and nuclear power appears to have been an attempt to re-create the pattern of the oil industry and at the same time to work toward a semi-monopoly over all fuel sources.

The companies' diversification moves also reflected four histor-ical developments. First, as the 1960s wore on, profit rates in the oil industry declined as increased competition from new firms drove prices down. Second, increased concern for environmental issues in the United States, Japan, and Western Europe led to considerable uncertainty as to which energy sources would be dominant in the future; given the state of technology and the politics of energy, coal and nuclear power were the most likely rivals to oil. Third, increasing nationalism in the oil-producing countries of the Middle East and North Africa made these coun-tries less dependable as future sources of supply, from the oil companies' point of view, even before the price increases and supply boycotts of 1973–1974. And fourth, there was increasing speculation, spurred by technical progress, that future supplies of petroleum might come increasingly from conversion of coal.

These developments worried the oil companies by threatening to deprive them of their monopolistic control over low-cost oil supplies and by threatening to make that control less profitable, if other energy sources gained a competitive advantage over oil. The companies' response was to widen their target from control of oil to control of virtually all commercial energy. One result is that oil companies now control 55 percent of the U.S. coal industry and 35 percent of the uranium industry.

The second largest U.S. coal company, Consolidation Coal, is owned by Conoco (itself a subsidiary of DuPont). The fifth largest coal company, Island Creek, is owned by Occidental Petroleum, which has become a multinational in coal as well as in oil, re-cently agreeing with the Chinese government to develop a mas-sive export-oriented coal mine in central China. Other oil company interests in coal include Standard of California's 20 per-cent stake in Amax, Standard of Ohio's ownership of Old Ben Coal Co., and Royal Dutch/Shell's ownership of the R & F Coal Co. In addition, several oil companies have their own direct coal operations, including Exxon (in both the United States and Colombia), Sunoco, Atlantic Richfield, and Kerr-McGee.

Similarly, uranium production in the United States and Canada is significantly controlled by oil companies. Gulf and Kerr-McGee have for years been among the major U.S. uranium producers, and in 1977 Atlantic Richfield bought the mining company Anaconda, which has large uranium interests. Exxon, Mobil, and Standard of California also have major uranium operations. In addition, the oil companies have moved toward vertical integration in the nuclear industry. Exxon has been involved in nuclear fuel fabrication as well as uranium mining, while Gulf is involved at all stages of the nuclear industry, from uranium mining to building nuclear reactors and reprocessing spent reactor fuel.

Outside the United States, the oil companies have taken a leading role in uranium. Royal Dutch/Shell has extensive exploration interests in South America, while a British Petroleum subsidiary is active in Australia. Getty Oil (recently acquired by Texaco) is the chief sponsor of the giant Jabiluka uranium deposit in Australia.

The recent collapse of the uranium market, in the face of increasing public concerns over nuclear safety and increasing evidence of the high real cost of nuclear power, along with the recession-generated slowdown in the growth of the coal market, has made the oil companies' moves into these alternative fuels less profitable than the companies expected.

New Energy Sources

The oil companies have also moved into newer energy sources such as geothermal power and solar energy. In the United States, Union Oil has taken a commanding lead in geothermal development, through its work in the Geysers field in California, the only commercial-scale geothermal plant in the country. Union Oil's work there, which has been heavily subsidized by the U.S. government, has put the company far ahead in geothermal research. In 1982 Union Oil began work on a similar project in Hawaii, using superheated steam from the still-active Kilauea volcano. Only two other countries have developed significant geothermal projects—Italy, where the work has been done by the state oil company Ente Nazionali Idrocarburi (ENI), and the Philippines, where both the government and private firms are involved.

The most promising energy growth industry for the foreseeable future, however, is solar power. Here, too, the big oil companies have jumped in—as always in an attempt to minimize risks and maximize profits from technological change. Contrary to the charges of some critics, we believe they are not out to suppress the development of solar power in order to protect their investments in oil. For one thing, in an infant industry such as solar this hardly appears possible, particularly since relatively little capital is needed to enter at this research-and-development stage; moreover, there is no such unity among the companies, and even if there were, any "conspiracy" to block solar power would likely be torpedoed by foreign competition, particularly from Japan.

Rather, the goal of each oil company is to "hedge its bets" by investing in solar power, hoping that it will be able to emerge in the future as one of the leading players in a vastly expanded and profitable solar industry. This investment is particularly attractive to the oil companies at present, since the Reagan administration, in its continual support of big business, has sharply reduced federal funding of solar research and development, thereby forcing smaller solar companies to turn to the oil companies for capital.

In any event, the fact is that in the United States, which at present leads the solar field, the four top solar firms are wholly owned by oil companies and two other major solar companies have important joint ventures with oil companies. Thus Exxon, Mobil, Standard Oil of Indiana, and Atlantic Richfield each own a leading solar company, while British Petroleum (through Sohio) and Royal Dutch/Shell (through Shell-U.S.) are hooked up with two other important solar firms.

Nonfuel Minerals

The massive profits generated by the oil companies in the post-1973 era have also led them to diversify out of the energy sector altogether, into metal mining. As the recent study *Big Oil's Move Into Mining* noted:

On the whole, petroleum companies became active in metals in the late 1970s and early 1980s, years after they got involved in coal and uranium. The oil companies had expanded significantly by this time, both in absolute terms and relative to the now far smaller mining firms. Metals producers had become more vulnerable to acquisitions because of slowed growth. Oil firms had little experience in primary or precious metals. For a petroleum company interested in these minerals, the purchase of an existing producer seemed more prudent and less expensive than efforts at internal development.

Among U.S. oil companies, for example, in the post-1973 period Standard of California bought 20 percent of Amax, the world's largest diversified minerals producer (but was rebuffed in its later attempt to gain full ownership), while Union Oil purchased a leading molybdenum company and Exxon bought a major Chilean copper mining company. Among major foreign oil company mining acquisitions were those by the French major, Elf-Aquitaine, of Le Nickel, a leading nickel producer, and Texasgulf, a diversified metals company, as well as the purchase by British Petroleum of another diversified mining company, Selection Trust.

The two largest takeovers, however, centered around the copper industry. In 1977 Atlantic Richfield, flush with cash from its part ownership of Alaska's newly producing giant oilfield at Prudhoe Bay, bought Anaconda, the third largest copper producer in the United States; in 1981 Sohio, which was catapulted into the big leagues by the same Alaskan oil, acquired Kennecott, the leading U.S. copper company. To date, owing to the failure of copper prices to rise from historic lows, these purchases have been disasters: Fortune has characterized them as two of the decade's seven worst mergers, and estimated that losses from them have reduced their new owners total profits by 20 to 25 percent. In 1984, Anaconda decided to sell off most of its remaining mineral properties.

The oil companies' ventures into other nonenergy businesses have fared nearly as badly as the mining acquisitions. Exxon's 1979 purchase of Reliance Electric Co., apparently on the basis of a revolutionary new electric motor, ultimately led to a write-off of hundreds of millions of dollars when the new motor failed to perform as promised. Exxon similarly has lost large amounts in its efforts to rival IBM, Xerox, and other office equipment companies in the sale of typewriters, copiers, and computers, while Mobil has rarely reported a profit from its Montgomery Ward retail chain.

Mergers in Oil

Faced with this nearly unbroken trend of losses in their nonoil ventures, the big oil companies turned at the end of the 1970s to the seemingly safer strategy of buying each other. As the cost of exploration increased, the oil companies found that it cost as much as $15–$20 per barrel to discover new reserves, while buying up other oil companies could effectively provide proven reserves at $5–$6 per barrel. This tend toward exploring for oil on Wall Street was fueled, in addition, by the existence of large pools of speculative capital, which by threatening unfriendly takeovers of some companies drove these firms' managements to seek more acceptable (i.e., oil industry) buyers. A further factor in the oil-merger mania was the relaxation of antitrust enforcement under the Reagan administration after 1981.

Virtually all the major oil companies were involved in such mergers. Shell Oil-U.S. started the trend in 1979 when it purchased Belridge Oil of California; Shell-U.S. itself then became, in 1984, the subject of a bid by its parent company, Royal Dutch/ Shell, to buy out its minority shareholders. Texaco bought Getty Oil, while Occidental was the winner in a bidding war for Cities Service. Finally, in the largest and most dramatic of the mergers, Standard Oil of California paid more than $10 billion in 1984 to buy one of the hitherto untouchable Big Seven itself, Gulf. All told, from 1979 to mid-1984, oil companies spent more than $35 billion to acquire each other.

Thus, at this stage in history the large international oil companies, which once begat other large oil companies and then alternately colluded and competed with them, are now voraciously devouring each other. Since all of this struggle has had the same basic goal for each company, namely the maximization of profits with minimization of risk, the new situation reflects developments not only in the oil industry, but in the world economy. The continuing stagnation and crisis of the international economy has generated in the business community a lack of confidence in long-run investment, and a consequent shift toward short-term financial speculation and takeovers of other companies. The manifestation of this crisis of confidence in the oil industry is the unwillingness to risk capital for new oil exploration and development and the preference for gaining new reserves through mergers and acquisitions.

As always, then, the problems and prospects of the international oil companies are linked closely to overall developments in the world polity and economy. In the next two chapters we shall examine the specific ways in which the fate of international oil companies has been linked to the fortunes of nation states involved in the continuing struggle for world economic and political power.

3

Trade and the Flag:
Anglo-American Oil Companies
and Their Home Governments

It has become commonplace in recent years to speak of the "global reach" of free-floating multinational corporations, thought to roam the world like lords of the jungle, immune from the influence of either their own stockholders or their home governments. This picture of untrammeled, independent corporations is, however, both misleading and dangerous. Throughout their history, and increasingly in the decade following the 1973–1974 oil-supply crisis, the international oil companies have been key instruments of national policy for their home governments. At the same time, these governments have played a crucial role in helping their oil companies to compete in the treacherous jungle of the international oil industry.

It is also important to recognize that despite the myth of the supranational corporation, one can speak meaningfully of "home governments." No matter how widespread the scope of their operations may be, each of the major international oil companies does, in fact, have a clearly defined home country—that is, where the majority of stock is held and hence to which profits flow. Thus, Exxon may operate in every country from Australia to Zambia and even has many subsidiaries that are legally incorporated outside the United States, but Exxon can quite accurately be considered a U.S. corporation, because the vast majority of its stock is owned by U.S. citizens. Shell Oil, on the other hand, is incorporated in and operates almost totally within the United States, but for all its efforts over many years to identify itself in the public mind as a U.S. company, Shell Oil is in fact a Dutch-British firm, because 69 percent of its stock has for many years been owned by Royal Dutch/Shell, which is in turn majority-owned by British and Dutch interests. Early in 1984, moreover, Royal Dutch/Shell began a tender offer to acquire the 31 percent of Shell oil that it did not already own, thus confirming the location of real ownership and control. Where the majority of stock ownership rests, the government will almost always prove to be a consistent active supporter of the company.

Why Governments Back the Companies

There are several reasons why the home governments support and assist their oil companies. First and most important, in many of the developed capitalist countries, particularly the United States and Great Britain, the major oil companies represent vast concentrations of economic power. And it has long been recognized that economic power gives rise to political power in a variety of ways, ranging from outright corruption of public officials to more subtle forms of influence; hence the remark by Charles Wilson, former Chairman of General Motors and Secretary of Defense in the Eisenhower Administration, that "what's good for General Motors [or Exxon] is good for the United States."

Second, the relationship between oil companies and their home governments has benefits for both sides. The companies' search for sources of crude oil and profits all over the world normally fits hand in glove with the governments' efforts to assure reliable supplies of oil for their military machines and their industries, as well as for popular consumption. For this reason alone governments support the expansion efforts of the oil companies. And if in the process of that expansion the oil companies earn huge profits that help the home country's balance of payments, this additional benefit simply provides a further basis for the continuing collaboration.

The mutual recognition of this symbiotic relationship has been made easier by the two-way flow of personnel that has taken place between the oil industry and those government agencies that deal with oil and foreign policy issues. The importance of this exchange of personnel has been recognized by the oil companies for many years. For example, shortly after World War II, Exxon's treasurer commented that

> as the largest producer, the largest source of capital, and the biggest contributor to the global mechanism, we [the United States] must set the pace and assume the responsibility of the majority stockholder in this corporation known as the world. . . . American private enterprise . . . may strike out and save its own position all over the world, or sit by and witness its own funeral. . . . As our country has begun to evolve its overall postwar foreign policy, private enterprise must begin to evolve its foreign and domestic policy, starting with the most important contribution it can make—"men in government."

This flow of people between the oil companies and the government in the 1950s has been detailed by oil scholar Robert Engler. Eisenhower's secretary of state, John Foster Dulles, had been a senior partner in Standard of New Jersey's main law firm; Herbert Hoover, Jr., a petroleum engineer and director of Union Oil, represented the State Department in the key secret negotiations dividing up Iran's oil in the 1950s; William Eddy, the first full-time U.S. resident minister to Saudi Arabia, became a consultant to the Arabian American Oil Company, handling governmental and public relations; Henry Holland, assistant secretary of state for inter-American affairs, represented oil groups operating in Latin America; Robert B. Anderson, who served Eisenhower as secretary of the navy, deputy secretary of defense, and treasury secretary, was a Texan active in oil production; and Walter Levy, the first chief of the European Cooperation Administration's Petroleum Branch and a staff representative for President Truman in the Iranian oil struggle, was a petroleum consultant whose clients included Standard of New Jersey, Caltex, and Shell. As Engler concluded: "Wherever there are consultants called in on national policy, the position and power of oil within the business community are sure to be recognized."

Close Ties in the 1970s

Continuing ties between the oil companies and the U.S. government came to light with the formation of the Federal Energy Office

(FEO) in the wake of the Arab oil boycott and the worldwide supply crisis in 1973–1974. In a story entitled "Links of Some Federal Energy Experts to Industry Raise Questions of Conflicts," the *Wall Street Journal* noted the case of a senior Exxon adviser on government affairs specializing in the Middle and Far East, who upon leaving Exxon in January 1974 had immediately joined the FEO as acting assistant administrator for foreign affairs; in this post he dealt with both foreign governments and the major U.S.-based oil companies, including Exxon. Moreover, before leaving Exxon, this executive had received a lump sum payment of tens of thousands of dollars from the company. A spokesperson for the company said that Exxon and other major oil companies make such payments so that "executives won't be discouraged from taking government positions."

Finally, we may note the conclusions of investigative reporter Robert Sherrill in his recent book *The Oil Follies of 1970–80:*

> As we have seen, those who presumably are the "regulators" of the industry often are alumni of the industry. Every time some political gadfly forced the Federal Energy Administration or the Department of Energy to divulge the professional background of its policy-making officials, the public learned that dozens—scores, hundreds—of them had migrated only recently from the warm nest of the oil industry. Did I mention that Senator James Abourezk had the General Accounting Office check the backgrounds of eleven agencies that had responsibilities over oil-industry affairs, and found two hundred and one former oil-company employees and affiliates in top-level positions in the federal agencies—and that didn't count the employees in two agencies that refused to answer the GAO's inquiry? Exxon, the largest oil company, was the one most frequently represented with former employees.
>
> (Tired of being embarrassed by such disclosures, the Department of Energy later put a ban on the release of such data either to politicians or to newsmen.)

In most of the major industrial countries outside the United States an even more direct relationship obtains between the oil companies and their home governments. Thus the British government for many years owned a majority interest in British Petroleum (BP) (although this holding has recently been reduced to less than 50 percent as a result of sales of BP shares to the public under Prime Minister Thatcher's "privatization" policy). Similarly, the French government for many years owned a one-third interest in the Compagnie Française des Petroles (CFP) (sometimes considered one of the eight major international oil companies), and in 1981 under the socialist government of President Mitterand raised this to a majority interest. In addition, the French government holds a controlling position in the Elf-ERAP petroleum group. In Italy, Ente Nazionali Idrocarburi (ENI) is a state oil corporation that has been particularly active in exploration in third world countries, with the aim of securing oil supplies for the home country. Deminex and Veba in West Germany, Spain's Hispanoil, and the Japanese Petroleum Development Corporation are additional examples of oil companies that are either owned or subsidized by their respective governments.

Oil and Government Power

In general terms, in fact, the Big Seven oil companies' rise in the twentieth century to their present dominant position in the industry is primarily a function of the growth of U.S. and British power in this period. Moreover, the ascendancy of U.S. over British companies in the post–World War II era similarly reflects the war-induced shifts in relative power between the two countries, marked by the break-up of the British Empire. The United States, it is true, had a great natural advantage over the rest of the world because of its large oil production prior to World War II, but the big growth in world oil production since then, as we have seen, has come outside the United States, particularly in the Middle East. Thus it is not merely the natural resources of the United States that have put companies based here at the forefront of the international oil industry, but rather the continuing use of the economic, political, and military power of the United States in support of the interests of these companies. (The corollary of this is illustrated by the general weakness of the state oil companies in third world countries that contain the bulk of the world's oil resources—a point to which we shall return in Chapter 5.)

The international oil companies have been dependent on state power from the very beginnings of the industry. The first major international challenger to the early dominant position of Rockefeller's Standard Oil was the "Royal Dutch Company for the Working of Petroleum Wells in the Netherlands Indies," the forerunner of Royal Dutch/Shell. This company was organized with Crown support in 1890 to exploit the oil of what is now Indonesia. To protect the infant company, the Netherlands government barred Standard Oil from entering the colony and sold the concession to Royal Dutch for $45,000, although it was worth almost $25 million. When Standard tried to gain control of Royal Dutch by buying up shares in the open market, the company quickly issued special shares that carried complete voting control and that could be held only by Dutch subjects, thereby ensuring its perpetuation as a Dutch company. The companies' own perceptions of their struggles as the equivalent of battles between nations is illustrated by the motto of the head of Royal Dutch during its period of continuous struggles with Standard Oil: "Either war everywhere, or peace everywhere." Although Standard Oil was unsuccessful in this battle, Rockefeller noted that "one of our greatest helpers has been the State Department in Washington. Our ambassadors and ministers and consuls have aided to push our way into new markets to the utmost corners of the world."

British Petroleum

British Petroleum, which originated in Iran at the beginning of the twentieth century as the Anglo-Persian Oil Company, owed its very existence, as well as its position in the industry, to British state power. British gunboats and troops were dispatched to protect the key British oil source, the D'Arcy concession of 1901, from England's archrival in Persia, Russia. When, after discovery of the world's largest oil field in the D'Arcy concession area in 1907, the concessionaires were ready to quit because of the huge financial burden of developing and marketing the oil, a British officer on the scene wrote to the British official in charge of the Persian Gulf region pleading: "Cannot Government be moved to prevent these fainthearted merchants, masquerading in top hats as pioneers of Empire, from losing what may be a great asset?"

To prevent the concession from lapsing, the British government induced Burmah Oil, a Scottish company, to launch the Anglo-Persian (later Anglo-Iranian) Oil Company with an investment capital of £2 million. Then, in 1914, Winston Churchill, at the time the British First Lord of the Admiralty, convinced the British government to invest another £2 million in Anglo-Persian and to take over majority control of the company (although day-to-day operations were left in the control of the company's nongovernmental shareholders and managers), telling Parliament that "we must become the owners, or at any rate the controllers at the source, of at least a proportion of the supply of natural oil which we require . . . and obtain our oil supply, so far as possible, from sources under British control, or British influence."

This was in line with the British government's overall aims for asserting its power in the Middle East: "For many years the policy of the Foreign Office, of the Admiralty, and of the Government of India has been to conserve independent English interests in the region of Persia, and, above all, to prevent this region falling under the control of the Shell or any other foreign or cosmopolitan company."

In the face of this British government-company alliance to preserve their monopoly position in Persia, the American government fought a continuing battle on behalf of U.S. companies to secure a foothold for them in the region. For example, in 1920 the secretary of state cabled to the British Foreign Office the State Department's position that "monopolization of the production of an essential raw material, such as petroleum, by means of exclusive concessions or other arrangements" was contrary to the Open Door policy of the United States. When in 1921 Standard Oil of New Jersey (now Exxon) applied for a concession in Persia, the Foreign Office in turn protested to the State Department. The continuing strength of British political and military influence is evident in the comment of a former U.S. ambassador that "the four vigorous efforts of friendly American oil companies in 1921, 1923, 1936, and 1944 to obtain oil concessions in Persia were all, in turn, unavailing despite the undoubted fact that no great power in recent times has ever enjoyed the general and spontaneous good will felt for Americans by Persians of all classes." Only after British power had been mortally wounded by World War II could British Petroleum's monopoly in Iran be broken.

Struggle in Iraq

A parallel struggle among the major Western powers for Middle East oil resources took place in Mesopotamia (now Iraq), which until the end of World War I was controlled by Turkey. The battle for Iraq's oil was particularly fierce because after World War I Standard Oil of New Jersey, which had traditionally emphasized foreign marketing, began to seek overseas production of crude oil as well. The British government, which had the main military power on the scene after Turkey was defeated, blocked Standard's (and Mobil's) efforts to secure exploration rights, while giving full support to the parallel efforts of Royal Dutch/Shell and British Petroleum. This caused Standard's president to comment, in a classic example of business patriotism: "British domination would be a greater menace to [Standard of] New Jersey's business than a German victory would have been." The British attempts to exclude the U.S. companies led to a sharp exchange of notes between the two governments, with the State Department telling the U.S. companies, according to a Gulf Oil official, "to go out and get it," and a British Foreign Office official claiming that "Washington officials began to think, talk, and write like Standard Oil officials."

The upshot was that, after years of complex negotiations, Iraq's oil was conceded in 1928 to a joint company in which British Petroleum, Royal Dutch/Shell, and CFP of France each got quarter shares, while Standard of New Jersey and Mobil shared the fourth quarter (with 5 percent of each company's share, including that of the Americans, going to the entrepreneur Gulbenkian, who played a key role as intermediary between the king and the companies). This settlement was part of the complex and historic "as-is" agreement negotiated between British Petroleum, Royal Dutch/Shell, and Standard of New Jersey to maintain their relative positions in world markets by controlling prices and production. Thus U.S. oil companies got their first toehold in the Middle East.

At about the same time the State Department helped produce an even more significant breakthrough for U.S. oil companies in the Persian Gulf. On the island of Bahrain, off the Saudi Arabian shore, Standard of California had acquired Gulf Oil's concession, which the latter could not use because Gulf was a party to the as-is agreement, which prevented any of the companies involved in the pact from going ahead unilaterally in the Persian Gulf region. Standard of California, however, which had not signed the as-is agreement, was then blocked by the British Colonial Office, which declared that only a British-managed company could have the Bahrain concession. The State Department once again, in the words of Harvey O'Connor, "entered the lists, jousting for the

Open Door," and a compromise was finally reached by which a Canadian subsidiary of Standard of California took over the concession, while the British government was given certain administrative rights.

Although Bahrain itself never became an important oil producer, it was the springboard for American companies' entry into two large and important concessions of the Middle East, Saudi Arabia and Kuwait. Standard of California, which found oil in Bahrain in 1932, acquired its first concession in Saudi Arabia in 1933, when it topped the Iraq Petroleum Company's offer of $45,000 to King Ibn Saud with its own bid of about $250,000 in gold sovereigns. For this amount, Standard of California got a sixty-year concession for all of Saudi Arabia's oil—a bargain on a par with the Dutch settlers' fabled seventeenth-century purchase of Manhattan Island from American Indians for $24. By 1936, Saudi Arabia looked so promising that Standard of California, which had no marketing outlets of its own for the vast quantities of crude oil that it was suddenly able to produce, sold a half-share of its Bahrain and Saudi properties to Texaco for $3 million in cash and an additional $18 million out of future earnings—another great bargain, this time for Texaco. The partnership between the two companies, which has since extended its operations to other areas of Africa, the Middle East, and Asia, notably including Indonesia's prolific oil fields, is known as Caltex.

Saudi Rivalry

American and British rivalry in Saudi Arabia and the Persian Gulf region increased in intensity during World War II. The war had brought Saudi production to a virtual standstill, but King Ibn Saud still needed revenues. Caltex tried to get the U.S. government to give him money in place of payments for the oil that was not being produced, and this was arranged at first by having the British pay the king out of U.S. lend-lease loan funds. However, because the U.S. companies and government feared that the British, who by then had sent a team of geologists into the country along with a military expedition, would use their position to try to monopolize access to Saudi oil supplies, from 1943 onward the lend-lease aid was given directly by the United States. The Saudi fear of British military power is indicated by King Ibn Saud's statement as to why Aramco was given a concession: "And His Majesty said, 'Well, I don't recall seeing many American warships around these waters!'" Interestingly, U.S. Petroleum administrator Harold Ickes and Navy Undersecretary William Bullitt wanted to set up a U.S. government corporation to take over Caltex's interest in Saudi Arabia, but the oil companies had this effort defeated in Congress (just as, in the 1970s, the companies were successful in defeating congressional efforts to set up a government oil corporation to act as a "benchmark" for gauging the effectiveness of the privately owned companies).

Additionally, the U.S. government, in its eagerness to advance the oil companies' interests in Saudi Arabia and to block any British moves into the area, provided huge amounts of very scarce steel after World War II so that Aramco could build a thousand-mile oil pipeline to the Mediterranean. Moreover, when the companies were under pressure to sharply increase their tax payments to King Ibn Saud under a new fifty-fifty profit-sharing agreement, the U.S. government stepped in to soften the blow. It established new tax rules that allowed the companies to credit these foreign tax payments against their tax obligations at home, so that the Saudi tax increase cost the companies virtually nothing; the U.S. Treasury, and in the long run the American taxpayer, footed the bill. Thus, while the oil companies' payments to Saudi Arabia increased from $66 million in 1950 to $110 million in 1951, their payments to the U.S. Treasury in the same period fell from $50 million to a mere $6 million.

While the struggle in Saudi Arabia ended in complete victory for the United States, in Kuwait compromises again had to be made with Britain. An independent entrepreneur had gained an oil concession in the 1920s covering all of Kuwait, and, after British Petroleum refused to buy up the concession, he offered it to Gulf. Having been blocked from Bahrain, Gulf readily accepted. Before Gulf could complete the purchase, however, the British government, which had sovereignty in Kuwait, intervened. British Petroleum had developed a new interest in Kuwait, and a struggle developed between the British and U.S. governments over which company was to get the concession. The American effort was headed by Andrew Mellon, then U.S. ambassador to Britain, whose family just happened to control Gulf Oil. In the event, the long tug of war ended in 1933 when Gulf and British Petroleum agreed on a fifty-fifty joint venture, called the Kuwait Oil Company, to take over the concession.

Other Battle Arenas

The Middle East was by no means the only battle arena, and the United States and Great Britain were not the only nations involved in the struggle to gain access to oil supplies in underdeveloped countries. A case in point is the Netherlands Indies (now Indonesia). There, after World War I, the Dutch government planned to turn German companies' concessions over to Royal Dutch/Shell, thus effectively locking out American companies. A U.S. State Department memo described the American reaction: "With a view to exerting further pressures on the Netherlands Government, the American Government took steps to block the issuance of further concessions to the Royal Dutch/Shell in public lands in the United States. The final result was that the New Jersey company [Exxon] was given additional producing concessions in the Indies which turned out to be some of the richest in the islands."

Similarly, in Mexico, which after World War I had become the world's second largest crude oil producer (after the United States), the U.S. government reacted strongly to the proposed new constitution of 1919, which nationalized subsurface mineral resources. This constitution would have harmed those U.S. oil companies that had received concessions in Mexico but had not yet started drilling. Opposing the constitutional provision, the U.S. government set out a concept of "minimum duty":

> Every nation has certain minimum duties to perform with regard to the treatment of foreigners, irrespective of its duties to its own citizens, and that in default of such performance it is the right of the foreign government to enter protest . . . one of the duties . . . is to refrain from measures resulting in confiscation of vested property rights of foreigners . . . [and if the Mexican courts failed to protect American companies' property rights] the Government of the United States must reserve to itself the consideration of the questions of interesting itself on behalf of American citizens.

In effect, the U.S. government was threatening armed intervention unless the oil companies' rights were restored. While the Mexican government eventually acceded to American pressure in 1928, the companies' victory was relatively short-lived, as their Mexican properties were completely nationalized in 1938. By that time, however, Mexican oil was no longer a major factor in the world market, and Franklin Delano Roosevelt, promoting his "Good Neighbor" image, declined to threaten military intervention.

In the case of France, the country's major international oil company, CFP, was actually set up in 1924 to hold France's share of former German holdings in the Ottoman Empire (even though two-thirds of CFP's stock was sold to private interests). In this case, since these holdings were war booty, it is self-evident that CFP owed its very existence to its home government's power.

Effect of World War II

World War II decisively altered the relative power relations among the major Western governments, a shift mirrored by changes in the relative position of each country's oil companies. The postwar strengthening of U.S. power relative to that of all other developed capitalist countries, combined with the upsurge of Soviet power and of nationalist and anti-imperialist sentiments in the third world, made it both inevitable and necessary for the U.S. government to push American oil companies to the fore. As we noted earlier, one evidence of this power was the rapid penetration of world energy markets by U.S. companies' oil, particularly in Europe, where the companies' efforts were aided by America's Marshall Plan loans.

U.S. power was exerted also in the opening up of the former European colonies to American oil interests. Beginning with the wartime lend-lease programs, and continuing with the Marshall Plan, the European powers, in order to receive military aid, had to accept the principle of the United States having "free and equal" access to all raw materials in their colonies. As a result of these kinds of pressures, American oil companies either got initial footholds or expanded their positions in many countries that had previously been the closed preserves of European capital. Thus,

Britain's monopoly of India's oil markets and Dutch domination of Indonesia's oil reserves were broken, while in the same period American companies got oil concessions in such places as French Tunisia, Portuguese Mozambique and Angola, and British-dominated Ethiopia.

The eagerness of Washington to promote American oil interests, even in countries such as Mexico and Bolivia that had earlier nationalized their oil industries, seemed unbounded. At the end of 1950 the U.S. ambassador to Bolivia reported triumphantly, if somewhat prematurely: "Since my arrival here, I have worked diligently on the project of throwing Bolivia's petroleum industry wide open to American private enterprise. . . . The whole land is now wide open for free American enterprise. Bolivia is, therefore, the world's first country to denationalize."

The most important third world arena for the capitalist countries' power struggle, however, was still the Middle East. The United States' basic aim was to pressure Britain out of as much of its Middle East oil holdings as possible, without making Britain so weak or uninterested in this vital area as to create a power vacuum that could be filled by the Soviets or by radical nationalism.

Crisis in Iran

As a result of the discoveries of vast oil reserves in Saudi Arabia and Kuwait, the U.S. companies' share of total Middle Eastern reserves had increased from only 10 percent in 1940 to one-third in 1945 and one-half in 1950. Yet the United States still coveted a share of Great Britain's 100-percent-controlled Iranian oil, which in 1950 made up over one-fifth of all Middle Eastern reserves. The opportunity for the U.S. government to do something to gain a position in Iran came in 1951, when an international crisis was precipitated by the Mossadegh government's nationalization of its oil industry.

Initially, Great Britain tried to restore the status quo by organizing a boycott of Iran's oil exports. The boycott, which was joined by all the major international oil companies and their home governments, was effective in cutting off virtually all of Iran's oil income. However, largely because the oil sector was a relatively autonomous island in the Iranian economy, affecting only a small part of the population, the boycott failed to achieve the British goal of overthrowing the Mossadegh government and/or restoring the nationalized properties to the British company.

Thus it took decisive action by the U.S. government in 1953 to overthrow the Mossadegh government. David Wise and Thomas Ross, while noting that "the British and American governments had together decided to mount an operation to overthrow Mossadegh," describe the crucial role of the U.S. Central Intelligence Agency:

> There is no doubt at all that the CIA organized and directed the 1953 coup that overthrew Premier Mohammed Mossadegh and kept Shah Mohammed Reza Pahlevi on his throne. But few Americans know that the coup that toppled the government was led by a CIA agent who was the grandson of President Theodore Roosevelt.
>
> Kermit "Kim" Roosevelt, also a seventh cousin of President Franklin D. Roosevelt, is still known as "Mr. Iran" around the CIA for his spectacular operation in Teheran. . . .
>
> One legend that grew up inside the CIA had it that Roosevelt, in the grand Rough Rider tradition, led the revolt against the weeping Mossadegh with a gun at the head of an Iranian tank commander as the column rolled into Teheran.
>
> A CIA man familiar with the Iran story characterized this as "a bit romantic" but said "Kim did run the operation in Teheran—but not from our embassy." He added admiringly: "It was a real James Bond operation."

The rewards to the United States from this naked exercise of American military might were substantial. Following the overthrow of the Iranian government, the oil properties were not simply restored to Anglo-Iranian, but instead a new corporation was given control of the properties. After prolonged negotiations, only 40 percent of the shares of this corporation went to British Petroleum, with another 40 percent going to the five U.S. majors (which in turn had to give one-eighth of their shares to sixteen other smaller U.S. companies); finally, of the remainder, Royal Dutch/Shell got 14 percent and CFP 6 percent.

As a minor footnote to the whole sordid Iranian affair, Kim Roosevelt later left the CIA and joined Gulf Oil as "government relations" director in its Washington office. Gulf named him a vice president in 1960. The major footnote was that the Iranian people were saddled for twenty-five more years with a U.S.-backed Shah whose increasingly barbaric regime was not toppled until the bloody uprising of the late 1970s.

The Decline of Britain

The crucial Iranian events of 1951–1953, along with the Suez Canal fiasco of 1956 (in which the United States failed to back an Anglo-French-Israeli invasion of Egypt following its nationalization of the canal, thereby helping to force the British into a humiliating withdrawal), also marked the end of overt U.S.-British rivalry over Middle Eastern oil affairs. Britain henceforth had to accept its junior-partner role in the area, and after that worked closely with the United States when action was necessary.

One example of joint action came in 1958 when a military group overthrew Iraq's feudal dictatorship and the entire Middle East was in ferment. American marines and a naval armada were dispatched by President Eisenhower, to Lebanon, where a civil war threatened, and British paratroopers landed in Jordan. The American government claimed that it sent in the Marines to protect Lebanon from "foreign agents"—the same pretext given by President Reagan twenty-five years later—but there is little question that oil interests were the underlying precipitating force. As Sir Anthony Eden wrote afterward: "Since the United Nations observers were already on the spot and proclaiming that the motives for Anglo-American intervention did not exist, it was rather more heinous."

Indeed, according to the *New York Herald Tribune*, at first the American government had given "strong consideration" to "military intervention to undo the coup in Iraq"; the State Department advised the U.S. ambassador to Lebanon that "marines, starting to land in Lebanon, might be used to aid loyal Iraqi troops to counterattack." Unfortunately for the United States, no "loyal" Iraqis could be found to act as tools for restoring a universally detested regime.

Nevertheless, the threat to the new Iraqi government was clear. The *New York Times* reported the decision of conferences between President Eisenhower, Secretary of State John Foster Dulles, and Foreign Secretary Lloyd of Britain: "Intervention will not be extended to Iraq as long as the revolutionary government in Iraq respects Western oil interests." As Robert Engler commented, "This gunboat diplomacy was clearly in line with the State Department's commitment to pipelines and profits." No other position could logically have been expected from Secretary of State

Dulles, who during the 1956 Suez crisis had declared to a secret meeting of top oil company executives and government officials regarding U.S. oil holdings in the Middle East that "nationalization of this kind of an asset . . . should call for international intervention."

Continuing the Policies

The continuity of American policy into the 1960s, even under the Kennedy administration, can be seen from events surrounding the 1963 overthrow of the new Iraqi government of Colonel Kassem. This military coup followed right on the heels of Kassem's announcement of the formation of a state oil company to exploit oil lands seized from the companies in 1961; it came four days after Kassem revealed an American note threatening Iraq with sanctions unless he changed his position. He did not, and the Paris weekly *l'Express* stated flatly that "the Iraqi coup was inspired by the CIA."

In the 1970s, the U.S. and British governments continued to work closely with the oil companies. The goals were, first, to slow down the attempts by oil-producing countries to renegotiate the old concession agreements, and then, following the price increases and the Arab oil embargo of 1973–1974, to prop up Middle East regimes that would support Western companies' interests and to intimidate those governments that took a more nationalistic stance. However, the effectiveness of these Anglo/American efforts to control the oil industry diminished after 1973. As Western oil economist Walter Levy commented:

> In the past, control over the international oil companies could be and was used as a political instrument by their home countries in their relationship to importing countries, such as the U.S. apparently did during the first Suez crisis or say for oil trade with Cuba, and so on. This possibility, to use the control over foreign oil for political-strategic purposes, is disappearing fast.

However, Levy's view appears to be overly pessimistic. The United States and the Western industrial countries have adopted a variety of strategies in the post-OPEC era to slow and even reverse this loss of control of such a key commodity. These have consisted of either unilateral actions by individual countries or, increasingly, multilateral actions working through international organizations such as the World Bank.

Insuring Investors

Underlying all of the efforts of the U.S. and other Western governments has been a generally perceived common interest in reducing the power of the Oil Producing Exporting Countries (OPEC) and particularly the Arab oil exporting countries. Aside from a continuing policy of Western intervention in the Middle East, whether outright or in conjunction with Israel, a key U.S. strategy has been both to try to expand the potential supply of oil outside of the OPEC countries and to make this non-OPEC oil more amenable to control by Western companies and governments. Toward this end a key tactic of the U.S. government has been the revitalization of the U.S. government's investor guarantee program, the Overseas Private Investment Corporation, or OPIC.

OPIC was set up many years ago to insure U.S. foreign investment, for a relatively small annual fee (about 1 percent of the foreign investment), against expropriatory action by host governments, inability to convert local currency into dollars, or war or insurrection. In the early 1970s OPIC virtually withdrew from the oil area, in part because of pressure from the anti-Vietnam war movement, which feared that if U.S. oil investment in Vietnam were insured, the United States would only become more deeply involved in the war there. By 1978, however, OPIC had revised its policy and was again heavily insuring investments for oil exploration and development.

What is particularly interesting about the revitalization of OPIC is that the new insurance policies reflected a strengthened U.S. government stand against "creeping expropriations" by third world governments. Thus, according to a 1978 OPIC document, "insurance coverage against expropriatory action covers more than government seizure of the project. It can also cover a variety of government actions which are arbitrary and which materially reduce the value of the investment." The same document goes on to give an example: "Thus, in [oil] production-sharing type agreements, any material unilateral change by the government in the percentage split would trigger a claim based on expropriatory action." Henceforth then, third world governments were put on notice that the United States was seeking to restore the sanctity, if not rigidity, of raw materials investment contracts; if an agreement called for the companies to get 40 percent of the oil produced and the country tried to reduce that share, it faced the grave danger of coming into conflict with OPIC, and behind it the U.S. government and the international financial community.

The World Bank

The multilateral effort to expand non-OPEC oil supplies has been spearheaded by the World Bank. Because the bank's role provides a classic case study of the evolution of Western oil tactics in response to changing conditions, it is worth examining in some detail.

Looked at in historical perspective, the World Bank's history regarding oil can be divided into three periods: (1) from its origins in World War II through the 1973 oil crisis (during which period it had a relatively consistent policy); (2) from 1973 through 1975–1976, when the World Bank appears to have been rethinking its policy in the light of changed oil industry conditions; and (3) from 1977 to date, when a new and controversial policy has emerged.

Through all three periods, the World Bank has generally been portrayed as an organization primarily devoted to promoting the economic development of third world countries by borrowing money in the developed countries and lending this money for projects in the developing countries. In fact, however, the bank's primary mission has always been, in the words of its Articles of Agreement, drawn up at the 1944 Bretton Woods conference, "to promote private investment."

Thus, the World Bank sees its main role in the world economy as providing loans to third world governments to supply the infrastructure necessary to attract private investment (e.g., roads, electric power, etc.) rather than loans for assisting a government's own enterprises. As a result, while the World Bank has always been a major lender to developing countries in the energy field, primarily for electricity production, before 1977 it had never lent them any money for petroleum exploration or production, preferring to reserve this highly profitable area to the international oil companies.

The World Bank also played an active role in attempting to affect oil policy in various third world countries. For example, it was widely known in the industry that in 1960 the World Bank commissioned and distributed among the governments of underdeveloped countries a study prepared by leading oil consultant Walter Levy that was strongly biased against active third world government participation in oil exploration in their countries. Again, it was well known that World Bank pressure helped deter the Indian government from undertaking offshore oil exploration in the early 1960s.

However, in the wake of the post-1973 concerns with worldwide oil supply and with the increased cost of oil imports, it seems clear that the World Bank and Western governments have gone through a reappraisal of their strategy. The new approach, which is still in the process of being defined, still emphasizes private investment, but recognizes, to a limited extent, the inevitability of a greater government presence in third world oil projects.

When in 1977 the World Bank first approved lending for oil exploration and development, it explicitly stated that there was an "expectation that relatively modest Bank financing would attract a much larger flow of investment from private sources." The World Bank also stated that "countries which lack the experience to do exploratory work themselves would be encouraged to enter into a contract with an interested foreign private or state-owned company and assisted in obtaining fair terms under an appropriate type of petroleum exploration and production agreement." (The bank did not say what "fair terms" might consist of.)

New Loan Programs

From 1977 through 1983 the World Bank announced loans for more than fifty oil projects, with a total loan commitment of over $5 billion. There seems little question that the program has been of value to some countries, such as India, which have obtained funds for development of much-needed energy supplies. Nevertheless, even in these cases it seems clear that this result is fundamentally an almost accidental by-product of the World Bank's push on behalf of Western countries to increase world oil supplies (as well as the bank's concern as a financial institution to help some of its biggest debtors, such as India, to repay their loans). A careful review of the bank's oil-lending program, which we have undertaken elsewhere, reveals that the major thrust of the program has been the support of the international oil companies and/ or the indigenous capitalist classes in the countries receiving the loans.

For example, recent oil loans to Argentina are described by the bank as aimed at "overcoming the financial and institutional constraints that are inhibiting increased participation by the Argentine private sector in the development of the country's promising hydrocarbon resources." The impact of the World Bank's assistance to Equatorial Guinea is summed up in more pithy language in a recent issue of *Business Week*, a journal not noted for its sympathy to the third world: "The government has been proposing far more liberal terms than oil companies typically encounter in other producing nations. 'It is written a little bit from hunger,' one U.S. source in Cameroon says of the government's petroleum law, which was actually put together by World Bank personnel."

Finally, it is important to be aware that even this limited and carefully channeled effort to allow some third world government input into oil exploration and development has generated considerable controversy within the industrial countries, particularly in the United States. On the one hand, the new bank policy appealed not only to weak oil powers such as Western Europe and Japan, which were most concerned with increasing world oil supplies, but also to weaker oil companies in the United States that did not have widespread oil reserves and also wanted the participation of the World Bank to ensure the stability of their investment. Initially, these forces were backed in the late 1970s by the Carter administration, which had less close ties than the Republicans to the largest oil companies and took a more "long-range" view of U.S. oil interests. Leading the opposition to the new policy was Exxon, the biggest of the U.S. oil companies, whose widespread oil reserves and enormous financial muscle made it much less needful of the World Bank's support, and much more fearful of the long-run dangers of encouraging third world government participation in this highly profitable sector; in addition, Exxon would be most threatened by large increases in third world oil supplies, which would endanger the OPEC price level. The 1980 election of the more big-oil-oriented and ideologically conservative Reagan administration shifted the government position toward that of Exxon, so that the bank's oil-lending program was scaled back from what had been proposed. The intensity of these struggles over expanding oil exploration has been muted at least temporarily by the present general oversupply of crude oil in the world.

The struggles over World Bank policy, however, should not obscure the basic thrust of its efforts, which are to strengthen the position of the industrial countries that control it. Divisions like this arise only on issues where there is divergence among the industrial powers. In this sense, the fight over World Bank policy reinforces the fundamental theme of this chapter: that the position and power of the industrial home countries of the international oil companies has been a crucial determinant of the fate of these companies. While this chapter has focused on the historical winners in the world oil struggle, the Anglo-American companies, in the next chapter we will examine the problems of the losers of continental Europe and Japan.

4

Caught in the Squeeze: Oil Strategies of Europe and Japan

In contrast to the United States and Great Britain, which either have been self-sufficient in oil or have had oil companies that controlled needed supplies abroad, the industrial countries of Western Europe and Japan have consistently lacked the luxury of such a protected position. Instead, historically they have been caught in a squeeze between their shortage of indigenous oil resources and the awesome power of the Anglo-American oil companies and their home governments to block these industrial countries from gaining their needed oil in the third world. In the last decade the loosening of the oil companies' stranglehold over the Organization of Petroleum Exporting Countries' (OPEC) supplies has simply meant replacement of the companies by OPEC governments as the second jaw of the vise.

Thus for nearly a century the industrial powers of Western Europe—particularly Germany, France, and Italy—and Japan have been engaged in a continuing struggle to secure their oil imports from far-off and, from their viewpoint, undependable sources of supply. In the early part of the century, this struggle took the form of support for each nation's companies in their efforts to win concessions in the Middle East. After the 1973–1974 oil-supply crisis, most of the European countries embarked on more direct, state-subsidized exploration. But whatever the mechanism, the basic problem for most of these countries remains the same: too much dependence on oil, and too few domestic oil resources.

61

Western Europe and Japan together consume about 18 million barrels of oil per day, or six times as much oil as they produce; only Norway and Great Britain, on the basis of their North Sea production, are net oil exporters, and for most countries domestic production is negligible. (Production and consumption for some of the major capitalist countries are shown in Table 4.1 in the Apprendix.)

This massive dependence on imported oil has, at various times in the past, been the source of both political and military confrontations among the Western powers. Wishing to avoid future conflict, most of these countries banded together after 1973 to devise a mutual protection group—the International Energy Agency (IEA)—which is in charge of setting up mechanisms for allocating crude oil when supplies are short. But this cooperative effort is still limited; most countries are hedging their bets by pursuing their own independent strategies for assuring the oil supplies as well; France, in fact, has never even formally joined the IEA. In this chapter we examine the historic strategy that each of the major petroleum-importing countries has pursued, as well as their likely future strategies.

The French Strategy

France, an early colonial power and a victor in the two world wars, was the most successful continental power in obtaining some access to the world's important oil-producing regions. France's first major interest in overseas oil supplies was a quarter share in Iraq's oil, which formed the basis for the Compagnie Française des Petroles (CFP), in which the French government retained a controlling interest. This quarter share in the Iraq Petroleum Company, which was half owned by British Petroleum and one-fourth owned by Royal Dutch/Shell, was wrested away from Germany in the peace settlement after World War I. As a by-product of CFP's interest in the Iraq Petroleum Company, and of the "Red Line" agreement of 1928 among the major oil companies, which guaranteed them equal access to new Middle East oil reserves, the French company also obtained quarter shares in subsequently granted concessions in Qatar and Abu Dhabi in the

Persian Gulf. And when Iran's oil was being redistributed among the companies after the Anglo-American-sponsored counter-revolution in 1953, CFP was able to acquire a 6 percent interest there as well.

In the marketing and distribution sector, CFP was further assisted by the actions of the French government. In 1929 that government decreed that the national company should henceforth have a minimum 25 percent share of the domestic French market for refined products. At present, CFP's refining operations process more than one million barrels per day, or over two-fifths of total French demand.

The most important recent role played by the French government has been through its direct control of the extensive French colonies in Africa and indirect influence after they achieved independence in the 1960s. This power, which was exercised so as to favor French oil companies and exclude British and American firms, provided CFP both with substantial crude oil supplies (first in Algeria and later in the Congo and the Ivory Coast) and with assured, predictable markets for refined products.

From the point of view of crude oil supplies, Algeria was the most significant French colony. Oil had been discovered there in the mid-1950s, and the presence of oil reserves so close to the home country was a major factor in France's stubborn unwillingness to agree to Algeria's independence.

Indeed, France's second major oil company, the wholly government-owned Entreprise des Récherches et d'Activités Petrolières (ERAP), was organized in 1939 specifically to explore for and develop Algerian oil. Thus, prior to Algerian independence in 1960, ERAP had the majority of concessions there, while CFP was in second place. Although their concessions have since been nationalized, the two companies still retain access to Algerian oil. They are also involved in exploration, production, refining, and distribution in almost all of the former French African colonies, including the Congo, Gabon, the Ivory Coast, Cameroon, and Senegal.

Despite the ability of France to obtain some access to oil in various countries, it never had much more than a foothold. French companies have never had a major share of any of the real bonanzas of the oil world, such as Saudi Arabia, Iran, or Venezuela. As a result, French-controlled crude oil production has never reached levels close to satisfying the country's rapidly growing oil consumption, particularly after World War II. Today, despite the expansion of CFP and ERAP into virtually all parts of the world, these companies' crude oil supplies and purchases account for less than three-fifths of overall French consumption.

Going it alone?

As a result of this constant shortfall in oil supplies, French companies and their government have tended to come into conflict with Anglo-American forces, especially in recent years. While the U.S. and British companies may have been willing to put up with CFP as a junior partner, holding a small share of Middle East production rights, this tolerance has decreased as France has attempted to expand its foothold in the oil-producing world. Two significant examples of this increased rivalry between France and the Anglo-American companies were, first, the struggle in the 1960s over which country's oil companies was to develop the rich Rumalia field in Iraq and, second, the decision of France to stay out of the International Energy Agency after 1974 and to attempt to make its own, separate deals with Arab governments.

The struggle in Iraq began in 1961, when the government took back from the Iraq Petroleum Company (IPC—by then a consortium of British Petroleum, Royal Dutch/Shell, Exxon, Mobil, and CFP) its concession in areas that were not then being exploited. (This area covered 99 percent of Iraq and included the rich North Rumaila oilfield, which had been discovered but was not yet in production). As a result, oil exploration in Iraq came to a standstill for more than five years, while the IPC member companies and the Iraqi government argued over the revocation of the concession. Then in early 1967, Ente Nazionali Idrocarburi (ENI), Italy's state oil company, began negotiating with the Iraqi government to acquire its own exploration and production rights to the disputed area. This in turn led the governments of the United States, Great Britain, the Netherlands, and France to put diplomatic pressure on the Italian government on behalf of their own companies.

In late 1967 France broke with the other countries represented in the IPC and began a two-pronged effort to improve its position in Iraq. First, ERAP negotiated an agreement to explore in all of Iraq's unproven areas, on behalf of the Iraqi state oil company. Soon thereafter, CFP itself, although it was a member of the IPC consortium, began separate negotiations with the Iraqi government for rights to exploit the North Rumalia field. CFP's action, as might be expected, was not looked on favorably by the other major oil companies and their home governments; it was seen as an indication that "de Gaulle has now decided that France can go it alone in oil affairs, and no longer needs to be cautious about stepping on Anglo-American toes."

France's independent stance in Iraq—beginning nearly a decade before the Organization of Petroleum Exporting Countries (OPEC) states took back full control of their oil industries—was a historic milestone in the international oil industry's history. The possible results were clearly forecast by John Buckley, executive editor of *Petroleum Intelligence Weekly*, in a 1967 talk to the New York Society of Petroleum Analysts.

> [Mr. Buckley] believes France may have shattered the foundations of the long-standing arrangements under which the international oil companies pump black gold throughout the world. . . .
>
> He said that when France's state-owned Entreprise de Récherches et d'Activités Petrolières took over confiscated concessions in Iraq, it broke faith with other consuming nations which had previously refused to support similar seizures by producing governments.
>
> E.R.A.P. has agreed to finance a search for oil in concession lands once owned by Iraq Petroleum Company. Mr. Buckley said that if France does this, other Arab nations are likely to break concession agreements that permit oil companies to reap big rewards. . . .
>
> Mr. Buckley said that the United States is now in danger of losing its control of Arab oil, which has put the nation in a very strong international position.

In the end, the French initiatives did not produce an agreement on the development of Rumaila, and after a 1968 coup the new Iraqi government decided to develop the field itself, with Soviet technical assistance.

France's role in Iraq

The importance of France's role was further shown in 1972, when Iraq nationalized another part of IPC's holdings. Most of the companies in the IPC consortium, together with their home governments, tried to organize a Western boycott of this nationalized oil, similar to the boycott that was organized against the Mossadegh government in Iran. The Soviet Union played the key role in undercutting this attempted boycott, both by agreeing to buy large amounts of the Iraqi crude and by providing sizable military and economic assistance. France, however, also agreed to buy large quantities of the Iraqi crude on a long-term basis, thus undermining Western unity. Despite CFP's ownership of almost one-fourth of the nationalized oil fields, France's overall interest, as a country highly dependent on Middle East crude oil imports, lay in a strategy of conciliation rather than confrontation with the Arab world.

The rewards for this strategy were not long in coming. The Iraqi government nationalized all U.S. and Dutch interests in IPC soon after the 1973 October war, leaving the French in a favored position. From the mid-1970s until the outbreak of the Iran-Iraq war in 1980, which reduced Iraq's oil exports to virtually nothing Iraq was France's major crude oil supplier, surpassing even Algeria.

France has continued to pursue its independent strategy throughout the 1970s and 1980s. One example of this independence is its refusal to join with the rest of the Western countries and Japan in the International Energy Agency's program for sharing oil among the industrial countries in the event of a future cutoff of supplies. In addition, the French government under both President Giscard d'Estaing and President François Mitterand has been among the most prominent suppliers of military equipment to Arab governments, often linking these weapons sales to assurances of continued oil supplies. Other examples of French independence include its willingness to negotiate oil exploration contracts with both Vietnam and China, well before other Western countries had gained a foothold in these areas.

The German Strategy

Underlying France's ability to pursue an independent oil strategy has been its military successes in two world wars and its continuing military capabilities. By comparison, Germany, as a result of its relatively late start in building a colonial empire and its military losses in two world wars, has been left in a position of severe oil shortage for many decades. German governments of varying political persuasions have tried to change this situation through diplomacy, military force, and economic influence, without much long-term success.

By the beginning of the twentieth century, the country, recently united under Bismarck and needing energy for its industrial revolution and for its growing military power, was already reaching out for new oil supplies. The German government used the Deutsche Bank of Berlin as its main instrument. As a means of attacking Standard Oil's virtual monopoly in the German market, the Deutsche Bank bought a 50 percent interest in Steau Romana, a major Rumanian oil producer (Rumania was at the time the leading producer outside of the United States). Standard Oil, as might be expected, resisted this challenge to its market dominance, and after an intense battle between the German and American firms, agreement was reached under which Standard accepted a limitation of its market share to a still-overwhelming 80 percent of the German market.

The Deutsche Bank, with the support of the German government, tried other approaches to gain greater German control of oil for the home market. Before World War I, for example, it tried to buy surplus crude oil from Texaco and Gulf (and even attempted to buy control of Gulf itself), but this effort was short-circuited by Standard Oil's purchase of their surpluses.

Because of the head start achieved by Standard Oil and Royal Dutch in securing overseas sources of supply, and because of the head start gained by other European powers, including England, France, and Belgium, in establishing colonial empires, Germany had been excluded from most of the parts of Asia and Africa that were most attractive for petroleum development (and, of course, from Latin America, which ever since the Monroe Doctrine had been seen by the U.S. government as its preserve). In the light of these restrictions on its activity in much of the world, Germany turned to the Middle East with particular eagerness.

When Germany's experts first investigated Middle East possibilities, around the turn of the century, they described Mesopotamia (now Iraq) as a "lake of petroleum." As an initial step toward gaining access to this high-grade resource, which at that time was outside any colonial spheres of influence, Germany built a railroad from the Bosphorus to Ankara, designed to be part of a Berlin-Baghdad-Bombay backbone for the still-to-be-acquired German empire. However, once the German government began negotiating with local Arab rulers for the rights to build an additional terminus for the railroad in the Persian Gulf, it ran into trouble. Fears of an expansionist Germany led the British government to assert greater authority in the area and to block the German bid.

The Deutsche Bank, in effect acting as the surrogate for the German government, continued, however, to seek some way of gaining access to Middle East oil. Finally, in 1914, the various governments involved agreed on the establishment of the Turkish Petroleum Company, with the Deutsche Bank having a one-fourth share, with an additional one-fourth going to Royal Dutch/Shell and one-half to British Petroleum. World War I, however, divided the partners and put Middle East oil resources up for grabs. One of the prizes of the war was the German quarter share in the renamed Iraq Petroleum Company, and, as we saw earlier, this share was handed over to a triumphant France in 1920.

Post–World War I policies

Beaten and bankrupt after World War I, Germany was hardly in a position to make any new gains in securing foreign oil supplies; the country remained basically a captive market for the American companies. Hitler's Third Reich tried to change the situation during World War II, and the planned conquest of Rumania, North Africa, and the Middle East would, in fact, have made Germany the world's dominant oil power. But Hitler's ultimate failure to win the war, far less achieve a position of dominance, left Germany even worse off.

When the United States became the overwhelming power after the war and used the Marshall Plan to promote the interests of the American oil companies, West Germany, an occupied country, was in no position to contest the issue. It could not even stand up against the forced shift from reliance on its own plentiful coal reserves to an almost complete dependence on imported oil—a dependence that persists to the present day. Even today West Germany is one of the weakest of the developed countries in terms of its reliance on imported oil and its lack of control of foreign oil reserves.

It was only in 1970 that the West German government finally took steps to establish a Germn-owned company (Deminex) to seek oil abroad. As of 1982, Deminex was importing only about 50,000 barrels per day, a tiny fraction of West Germany's requirements. Although the company planned to increase this amount from its involvement in third world exploration and production projects to more than 200,000 barrels per day by 1990, this would still be less than 10 percent of German consumption. The German refining industry is still dominated by Exxon, Royal Dutch/Shell, British Petroleum, and Mobil, which together have nearly two-thirds of the country's refinery capacity.

The Italian Strategy

Like Germany, Italy was on the losing side in World War II, and hence lost virtually all access to colonial sources of crude oil supplies. But Italy has pursued a much more aggressive policy to gain access to oil, using its state oil company vigorously, and accepting contract terms that are sometimes more favorable to the host country than those that the major American and British oil companies are willing to negotiate.

As a result, ENI, Italy's state oil company, has its own production of more than 300,000 barrels per day abroad plus purchase contracts for foreign oil that provide another 600,000 barrels per day. Thus ENI supplies nearly half of Italy's oil import needs, in contrast to the situation in West Germany, where German-owned enterprises supply only a small fraction of the domestic market.

This relatively strong position has not always obtained. Historically, Italy was handicapped by lack of indigenous energy resources of any kind, except for some hydroelectric power and recently developed geothermal resources. And even though Italy was on the winning side in World War I, it was not able to get any of Germany's share of Iraq's large potential oil reserves. Then in 1926, long before German governments began supporting foreign oil exploration, Mussolini's fascist regime formed a state-owned company, AGIP (which is today the oil exploration, production, and marketing component of ENI), with a mandate to explore for oil both in Italy and abroad.

Before World War II, however, AGIP had relatively little success, obtaining some medium-sized oil companies in Rumania and gaining access to some Albanian crude oil. AGIP also attempted to gain a foothold in the rich Middle Eastern fields, through acquisition of a company that held a small concession in Iraq. Even this foothold, however, was lost as a result of the Italian invasion of Ethiopia in 1936. Mussolini's militarism, reflected in the Ethiopian conquest, made the British eager to force Italy out of the critical Middle East area. Since Italy lacked the financial wherewithal to support a big exploration effort in Iraq, and thus to meet the requirements for holding on to its concession, AGIP was in effect ordered to accept IPC's offer to buy it out.

AGIP did succeed in building up in Italy a strong oil-product distribution network based on imports, however, and by 1939 had one-quarter of the domestic market (its main rivals being Exxon and Royal Dutch/Shell). In addition, another subsidiary of ENI established some nationally owned refining capacity in the country. What was missing was an assured supply of crude oil, under national control. ENI chairman Enrico Mattei, who took over leadership of the state company in 1946 and rapidly became known as one of the most dynamic figures in the international oil industry, was successful in finding sizable amounts of natural gas within Italy, in the Po Valley, but he did not find equivalent amounts of crude oil at home. His subsequent vigorous efforts to obtain foreign crude oil, and the repercussions that these efforts caused within the international oil industry, make Mattei's strategy worth noting.

ENI: caught in a squeeze

ENI's primary mission, as an arm of the Italian government, was to provide low-cost energy for Italy. Under Mattei's leadership, the company attempted both to keep down the price of imported crude oil and at the same time to acquire a significant share in direct ownership of overseas crude oil for Italy by offering more attractive deals to the governments of the oil-producing countries than were being offered by the big Anglo-American oil companies. Thus in the 1950s, ENI bought large amounts of low-priced "barter oil" from the Soviet Union, paying in products and services rather than dollars. Most significantly, in its efforts to secure access to overseas oil reserves, ENI gave up the standard fifty-fifty profit split between the oil companies and the host governments of the oil-producing countries and offered a seventy-five–twenty-five split in favor of the governments.

Unfortunately for Italy, Mattei's ENI never actually discovered very much crude oil abroad, while the country's oil consumption, like that of the other Western European countries, expanded rapidly. By 1962, when Mattei died in a suspicious plane crash, ENI was producing only a minor part of Italy's oil needs. After Mattei's death, ENI seems to have become much more conciliatory in its dealings with the big international oil companies.

As *Petroleum Intelligence Weekly* noted in 1965: "Since Mattei's death, his successor, Eugenio Cefis, has established a working rapport with the big internationals and crude oil purchase deals have been negotiated by the crude-short Italian company with both Esso and Gulf Oil."

Perhaps coincidentally, ENI's overseas production has also increased. In the 1980s it held interests in oil exploration and production in most of the African producing countries, frequently as part of a consortium with American independents Phillips and Getty (acquired by Texaco in 1984) and Spain's state oil company, Hispanoil.

Despite some improvement in its exploration record in the 1970s, however, ENI still has not found any foreign reserves comparable to the giant Middle East fields and can bring home only half of Italy's crude oil requirements. Italy is plagued by a chronically weak currency, and unless it can secure significantly larger crude oil supply sources, the country will remain caught in a squeeze between the forces of the major international oil companies and their home governments, on the one hand, and the oil-producing countries on the other; it must depend on one or the other, if not both, for needed energy. This makes it virtually impossible for Italy to be more than a passive spectator as events unfold that will affect the very lifeblood of its economy.

The Japanese Strategy

If Italy's position in energy is weak, consider the plight of Japan. Of all the major capitalist industrial countries, Japan is the most thoroughly dependent on imported energy. While the Marshall Plan's emphasis on shifting Europe from coal to oil was a major factor in increasing European reliance on oil imports, Japan, since the beginning of its industrialization in the 1860s, had always sought overseas energy sources; the lure of coal in Manchuria and oil in Southeast Asia were probably the most important reasons for the Japanese invasions of these regions in the 1930s and 1940s. Today Japan remains extremely dependent on imported oil from the Persian Gulf and Indonesia. The uncertainty of its energy supplies is among the most significant features determining Japan's foreign policy.

Historically Japan's energy economy was based primarily on coal and on hydroelectricity, with some oil imported by the major international oil companies. Before World War II Japan, like Germany and Italy, was effectively excluded from the world's major oil-producing areas. Like them, it hoped to gain from its war effort entry into such supply sources as Indonesia and Burma, but, of course, these hopes were shattered by its decisive defeat.

During the American military occupation after the war, the international oil companies, with the support of the U.S. occupation authorities, helped turn Japan, like Western Europe, from a primarily coal-consuming country to an oil-based one. Oil's share in total energy consumption increased from less than one-tenth in 1950 to more than three-fifths today. The companies, which primarily saw Japan as a potential outlet for their low-cost and high-profit Middle East and Indonesian crude oil, joined together with Japanese business interests to build up a huge indigenous refinery industry. The rapid rise to power of American companies in particular in the Japanese market is seen from their supplying over three-fifths of Japan's crude oil by the mid-1960s.

Japan begins to explore

In response to the steadily increasing dependence on imported crude oil, Japanese companies, with strong government support, tried to gain their own concessions in important oil-producing areas. The most significant early acquisition was the 1958 concession obtained by a private Japanese company (Arabian Oil) from Saudi Arabia and Kuwait to explore in the "neutral zone" between the two countries. This concession was obtained by offering better terms to the governments than the major oil companies' traditional fifty-fifty profit split. The Japanese soon found oil in the concession and with the assistance of the Japanese government began shipping it to Japanese refineries in competition with the majors' crude oil. The relatively poor quality of this oil (it has a high sulfur content), however, combined with the rapidly swelling Japanese demand, ensured the continued dominance of the majors in supplying Japan's crude oil needs.

More recently, the Japanese government has sponsored creation of a state-subsidized company, the Japan Oil Development Corporation (JODC), in which the government and the major Japanese industrial companies (Sumitomo, Mitsui, Mitsubishi, etc.) hold equal shares. JODC has acquired exploration rights in Latin America, Africa, and especially Southeast Asia, and was one of the first companies to sign exploration agreements with China. In addition, Japanese interests have acquired a major share of Abu Dhabi's production.

Japan also has been particularly active in using barter arrangements and counter-trade (in which financing for oilfield development is secured by promises to export the oil), both with Middle Eastern countries and with the Soviet Union. Japanese banks, for example, provided most of the funds for the huge East Siberian oil and gas development projects, under counter-trade arrangements, and Japanese firms have supplied factories to Middle Eastern countries in exchange for oil, as in the case of a billion-dollar petrochemical plant for Iran. All in all, in view of its limited nonoil energy sources, Japan is likely to remain the most dependent of the industrial powers on imported oil for the rest of the twentieth century.

Common Problems

In conclusion, the industrialized countries discussed in this chapter have one main thing in common: they have lost out to the United States and Great Britain in the oil struggle of the twentieth century. Whether this has happened because they lost world wars or because of their relative economic and military weakness, for each country the result has been no alternative but to rely on foreign-controlled oil supplies (see Table 4.1 in the Appendix).

For a time during the 1960s, however, the significance of this reliance was hidden by the low crude oil prices that prevailed. As the economies of the oil-importing industrial countries expanded during the long boom period of the 1960s, and as these countries' exports increased even faster than their domestic production, the rising oil-import bill could easily be financed. Oil imports generally were a manageable 10–15 percent of total export revenues for these developed countries during this period.

This comfortable situation was reversed almost overnight after the 1973 war in the Middle East, when oil prices skyrocketed. Suddenly, the oil-deficit position of the non-Anglo-American industrial countries was revealed as their Achilles' heel. Because the United States imported relatively less oil than these countries, and also had the foreign exchange benefits of the greatly increased profits of its international oil companies, currency speculators and investors rushed to dump their marks, yen, and francs in favor of dollars. Only large-scale borrowing by Western Europe and Japan prevented their foreign exchange reserves, which had been painfully built up over more than two decades of prosperity, from disappearing almost overnight.

Moreover, the sums of money these developed countries have been required to pay for their oil imports since 1973 have imposed a continuing strain. Oil imports typically have accounted for some 15 to 20 percent of total imports in France and Germany, 20 to 25 percent in Italy, and 30 to 35 percent in Japan. Nonetheless, these industrial countries have, by and large, managed to cope with the increased cost of oil imports. Among the reasons for their relative success were their ability to increase the prices of the industrial goods they export, and their greatly increased exports to OPEC countries.

Despite all the dramatic changes that have taken place in the world in the twentieth century, the industrial countries of Western Europe and Japan still feel oil to be their Achilles' heel. Lacking indigenous supplies, they continue to be caught in the grip of forces beyond their control. Although historically they have been able to adapt to this weak position, the price has been relegation to a junior role not only in the oil industry but in the industrial capitalist world as a whole. Barring a discovery of large-scale indigenous oil resources, which seems highly unlikely given that their small land and offshore areas have been already highly explored, Western Europe and Japan can only continue to navigate the perilous seas of the oil epoch, hoping to sail relatively smoothly into a post-oil energy era.

5

Rich But Not Powerful:
The Oil-Exporting Countries

A relative handful of countries has always produced most of the oil moving in international trade. Since 1973 the world's attention has focused on the latest group, the Organization of Petroleum Exporting Countries (OPEC), and attributed to it great power. In reality, however, while a group such as OPEC may have its moment in the sun, historically oil-exporting countries rise and decline relatively quickly. By contrast, what remains constant is the collective power of the international oil companies and their home governments in the West. Indeed, as we shall try to show, it is the very fact that the oil-exporting countries have to operate within the overall context of enormous Western economic, political, and military power that makes it extremely difficult for the oil exporters to restructure the international oil industry.

In 1973 the eleven members of OPEC produced about two-thirds of the capitalist world's crude oil, and accounted for more than 70 percent of all crude oil traded internationally. By the early 1980s these ratios had declined to about 40 percent and 55 percent, respectively, while OPEC members' shares remained relatively fixed. By far the most important exporter was Saudi Arabia, which accounted for about 40 percent of all OPEC production, and acted as "swing producer" in response to changes in world oil demand (i.e., the other OPEC countries produced a relatively constant amount, while the Saudis increased their output when world demand rose and cut back their production when world demand declined). The other large OPEC producers were Iran,

Iraq, Abu Dhabi, and Kuwait in the Middle East; Nigeria, Libya, and Algeria in North Africa; and Venezuela and Indonesia (other major oil exporters not in OPEC were the Soviet Union, Mexico, Norway, and Great Britain).

Although the Western world has frequently appeared to shudder with fear at this "new" concentration of production in the OPEC countries, in reality concentration of production has been a fact of life in the oil industry from its very beginnings. Until 1880, over 85 percent of world oil production was in the United States; with the rise of production in Russia in the next twenty years that country's share jumped to one-half while the U.S. share fell to two-fifths—still, over nine-tenths in two countries, a level of concentration that would make OPEC's mouth water. From 1900 to 1915 the United States quadrupled production and regained the lead, with its world share rising to 65 percent while stagnating Russian production caused its share to drop to 15 percent. In the next five years production catapulted in Mexico, which captured a 10 percent share of world production, even while the U.S. share rose to 70 percent.

Thus the United States clearly dominated crude oil production through 1950. This historic pattern of U.S. dominance, combined with shifting patterns of other countries rising and falling as producers and exporters, reflected two basic facts of life of the oil industry. First, the industry began in the United States, which had large reserves and provided a large market. Second, the international oil companies or their home governments were continuously on the lookout for new sources of low-cost crude oil that could be pumped out quickly for huge profits. The approach is graphically described by Harvey O'Connor, writing about Mexico's brief moment in the oil sun:

> The American and British pioneers in Mexican oil were true buccaneers, bent on plunder only. The great wells which astonished the world were for the most part shallow and their drilling was primitive indeed. The Dos Bocas well that burnt itself out was not even cemented, and the fires in the boilers were not extinguished when the great column of oil and gas erupted. The well ran 50,000 to 100,000 barrels a day, in a cloud that covered the Mexican sky as it burned. The famous Potrero del Llano No. 4 ran wild for eight months for lack of decent drilling procedures. After being controlled, it produced 117 million barrels. . . . Such wells truly earned the name of "fabulous," for nothing like them had ever been

known—not in Pennsylvania, nor in Texas and Oklahoma. But they were plundered of their superficial wealth, while the gas was burnt to the sky.

Company Dominance

The dominance of the Anglo-American oil companies and their home governments over the oil exporters is amply demonstrated by the early-twentieth-century experience of the leading members of OPEC. The combination of Western power and greedy and corrupt local regimes was normally sufficient to ensure such a situation. In the case of Iran, for example, George Stocking, an expert on oil in the Middle East, notes that

> while the Persian shahs of the nineteenth century customarily were neither accountable to nor held in restraint by any coherent social group, they were not equally free from foreign influence. . . . Russia and Great Britain settled their rivalry in Persia by signing a treaty, the Anglo-Russian Convention of 1907, which, while piously recognizing Persian integrity and independence, divided the country into spheres of Russian and British influence.

Even before that, in 1901 the Persian government granted the key oil concession to the British-owned Anglo-Persian Oil Company (now British Petroleum). This amazing concession covered almost 500 thousand square miles, or four-fifths of the country, and the oil companies were granted virtually free hand, including exemption from all taxes. In exchange for this enormous benefit, the Shah and his cronies received £20 thousand and £50 thousand worth of stock in a new oil company formed to exploit the concession. In 1909 the Shah granted a pipeline right-of-way and sold Abadan island to Anglo-Persian for a similar pittance. The result of these corrupt practices could be seen from the fact that as late as 1947 the Persian government's revenues from oil were less than one-tenth of the value of oil produced.

Similar situations were virtually universal. In Iraq, Great Britain was the thinly veiled power behind the throne that granted the key concession in 1925. This concession covered most of the country and was to run until the end of the twentieth century, with payment to be an almost nominal sum of four shillings per ton of crude oil produced. For this enormous giveaway, King Faisal got a "little present" of £40 thousand.

In Saudi Arabia the companies apparently fared even better, with Standard of California in 1933 obtaining the concession to what turned out to be the world's greatest oil bonanza by payment of a mere £50 thousand to King Ibn Saud; moreover, Socal's negotiator wrote to the U.S. State Department that the Saudi "government is not publishing details of the loans and payments, as it wishes to avoid the criticism of those who might say it should have obtained terms equal to the Iraq and Persian governments."

In Venezuela most of the key concessions were given away from 1908 to 1935 by dictator General Juan Gomez, who was backed by the U.S. government and, according to O'Connor, "protected by perhaps the most savage set of cut-throats to be found in all the sad history of Latin America . . . he built up the most effective police state in America, complete with dungeons and political prisoners chained to grills weighing 100 pounds." Edwin Lieuwen, a leading authority on Venezuela's oil history, has noted that "fraud and deception, chicanery and double-dealing, were the rules of the game. . . . Three big American companies [Exxon, Standard of Indiana, and Gulf] obtained their lucrative leases in the corrupt-concessions era of the Gomez regime. Shell rested on its plentiful grants received earlier." One example of largess to Shell was that in 1913 it received a concession covering 4,000 square miles in the highly productive Lake Maracaibo district on which taxes were to be limited to a flat $380,000 per year.

Changes Since 1973

For many observers, the OPEC countries since 1973 have so revolutionized the international oil industry that they are the dominant power in the industry, holding the international oil companies and their home governments at their mercy. And, in fact, no one can deny that in these years there have been great changes in the oil industry. From 1972 to 1982 the seven majors' share of total nonsocialist crude oil production dropped from three-fifths to two-fifths (and this includes crude oil they purchase under "buy-back" arrangements with state oil companies in producing countries). With the OPEC countries' takeover of crude oil production, pricing, and taxation, their revenues have increased enormously, from $8 billion in 1970 to $90 billion in 1974 and $200 billion in 1982. Yet a careful examination of the events leading up to 1973 and following thereafter will reveal the very important ways in which the international oil companies still remain dominant in the industry, as well as the failure of the "OPEC revolution" to initiate what many people expected would be a period of rapid and relatively widespread economic development for its member countries.

We may summarize in broad strokes one key aspect of the power balance in the oil industry in the post–World War II period by examining the rough division of profits from crude oil production. By around 1950 the pittances given to governments of oil-producing third world countries had been increased to fifty-fifty profit shares (aided, as we have seen, by changes in U.S. income tax policy that shifted the burden from the companies to the U.S. taxpayer). The oil companies' profit rate on investment under these conditions was still so enormously high that it encouraged newcomers to enter the industry on a large scale in the 1950s and 1960s, particularly in the oil-rich Middle East and North Africa. As a result of the competitive pressures, all through the 1960s the market price of crude oil fell steadily, from about $2 per barrel for Arabian Light to $1.25 per barrel in 1969. Moreover, since OPEC, which was organized in 1960, had managed to maintain throughout the decade a formula calculating its share of profits as if the earlier, higher market price still prevailed, all of the market price reductions came fully out of the profits of the companies. Thus by 1969 the companies' profit per barrel on Arabian Light had been reduced to about $.20, and the government's share of profits had increased to over 80 percent.

Although the companies' profit rate on investment was still quite high, the trend was clearly not satisfactory to the major companies. Indeed, the dangers to the majors of this trend were pointed up in a famous price projection made by Professor M. A. Adelman, an exponent of the "Chicago school" of competitive economic theory. Adelman foresaw that competitive pressures would in the 1970s push the market price of oil down toward $1 per barrel or lower, virtually wiping out oil company profits.

As the reader is well aware, with oil prices in the late 1970s reaching $24 per barrel, this projection ranks with Herbert Hoover's "Prosperity is around the corner" as among the worst in history. Even by mid-1973 the price of Arabian Light had doubled to $2.50 per barrel (and company profits had quadrupled to about $.80 per barrel).

Reasons for the Shift

The key immediate causes of the price reversal from 1969 through 1973 appear to have been, first, the aggressive policy toward the oil companies adopted by the new government of Colonel Qaddafi in Libya, and second, the tightening supply/demand situation in this period. With the Libyan government threat to reduce the oil companies' production if they did not pay it more per barrel acting as a spur to other OPEC countries, a series of complex international negotiations took place in 1971–1972 that resulted in increases in the market price of OPEC oil. While the companies were thus enabled to sharply increase their profits, on the negative side for the first time the countries obtained the right to purchase "participation shares" in the companies' oil production, with the promise of getting a majority share in the early 1980s.

All this, of course, was eclipsed by the enormous changes that took place in the wake of the October 1973 war between Israel and the Arab world. The resulting cutback in Arab oil production and the embargo on sales to the United States sent crude oil prices skyrocketing, and enabled the OPEC countries to take control of crude oil pricing from the companies; essentially this was because in this period of panicked reaction to oil shortages it became clear to the producing countries that they had the upper hand in bargaining power and could sell directly to the importing countries if the companies balked at having their role usurped. Thus, in three months the price of Arabian Light quadrupled to $11 per barrel, a level at which it basically remained until the Iranian crisis of 1978–1979 allowed another doubling of price.

Moreover, the victory of OPEC in the pricing area dramatically demonstrated its collective power, and allowed the OPEC governments to leapfrog the plans for gradual transfer of majority ownership in the oil fields and take over completely in the 1970s. At this point, the combination of the transfer of control of crude oil production and of crude oil pricing appeared to some observers to give OPEC all the power, leaving the companies with none. This assessment was superficially supported by the fact that in general OPEC was able to obtain 95 percent or more of crude oil profits, leaving the companies with per barrel profits under $1, which were viewed as "service fees" for the companies' "know-how."

Company Responses

That this view of OPEC's relative power vis-à-vis the oil companies and their home governments was and is incorrect could be predicted by any oil analyst with some sense of the history discussed earlier. It is not without good reason that the oil companies, which are the most enormous concentrations of economic and political power in the Western world, have "nine lives," and to take the feline metaphor one step further, have many ways to "skin the cat." In the following, we will briefly discuss the ways in which the oil companies and the Western governments have been able to "re-tilt" the balance of power in their direction.

One very important factor has been the historic ability of the oil companies to shift their efforts from one group of countries to another in their pursuit of secure and profitable sources of crude oil. This tendency was greatly increased by the OPEC actions of the early 1970s, which made OPEC oil less reliable and less profitable than non-OPEC oil. Thus the companies pushed hard in the 1970s to find and develop oil production in such politically safe areas as Alaska and the North Sea. The incentive for such production was epitomized by the case of Alaska, where by the end of the decade company profits reached nearly $10 per barrel, or ten to twenty times the level in OPEC countries.

A second factor that reduced OPEC's power fairly quickly was the combination of recession in the economies of the capitalist world and the effect of conservation on world oil consumption. (Although the recession was blamed on the oil price increases, in fact they played only a minor role.) As a result, total world oil consumption basically stagnated in the 1973–1979 period, and then fell by about one-fifth through 1982.

The deterioration in the relative supply/demand position for oil has been accelerated by the attempt of OPEC to protect the price of oil by accepting (necessarily) that when world demand fell, it would allow non-OPEC countries to continue producing at their oil levels, while OPEC member countries would reduce their output. One result of this has been the steady decline in OPEC's share of capitalist world crude oil production, from 67 percent in 1973 to 40 percent in 1983. Moreover, the attempt to apportion the declining share among OPEC members has created serious strains within OPEC. The basic problem for OPEC is that while the organization collectively may target national output levels, in times of low demand, or "glut" conditions, the companies can rather easily thwart national output targets with their diversified supply sources in many countries.

Oil and National Development

Having examined the limitations of the oil-exporting countries' power within the international oil industry, we can now turn to an assessment of the impact of petroleum wealth on the lives of their people. Here too we shall see that the much-vaunted riches generated by crude oil production have done surprisingly little for the masses of people. The principal problem is that in most of these countries there have not been developed new economic, political, and social structures that would permit the harnessing of the oil resources in a positive way on a wide scale.

The failure of the hopes, or perhaps more accurately the illusions, that the enormous increase in OPEC revenues after 1973 would bring a new life to these impoverished countries can best be seen by an examination of developments in the Persian Gulf countries. After all, it should always be recalled that not all oil-exporting third world countries have small populations—Nigeria and Indonesia with their near 100 million populations and Mexico with its 50 million being the most important exceptions. For these larger countries it might be argued that it is unreasonable to expect that oil wealth could completely transform them. But for the Persian Gulf countries, with their tiny populations, clearly the enormous inflows of oil revenues could have had an enormous positive impact. Hence, these countries are the best laboratory case studies to see how and why the potential of oil wealth has not materialized.

The small Persian Gulf oil-exporting countries—Saudi Arabia, Kuwait, the United Arab Emirates, Oman, Bahrain, and Qatar—together have a population on the order of only 10 million people. Yet in recent years they have received over half of the oil revenues of OPEC as a whole. Saudi Arabia alone has collected almost 40 percent of OPEC oil revenues, and from 1973 to 1982 its accumulated oil revenues amounted to almost $500 billion—$50,000 for every single person in the country. What has been the result of this unprecedented accumulation of oil wealth in the Persian Gulf? Superficially at least, all is rosy, and in popular mythology the people of these "privileged" countries are like the winners of lottery tickets who overnight have been catapulted into the ranks of the wealthy. This mythology is aided and abetted by comparisons among countries based on one of the most misleading economic statistics, "per capita income," which is calculated by mechanically dividing total income for a country by its total population. On the basis of this average income per person "calculation," the small Persian Gulf oil exporters rank on a par with the most advanced of the Western industrial countries.

One problem with these data, of course, is that in reality the distribution of income in the Persian Gulf countries is extremely unbalanced, with a relative handful receiving astronomical amounts and the great majority a relative pittance. Reflecting at least partly the fact that these unequal income distributions are highly charged politically, there are no published data available. Nevertheless, there are some measures of social welfare published that indicate a considerable gap between average social indicators in the Persian Gulf and those in the Western industrial countries. For example, life expectancy is 55 years in Saudi Arabia, 63 years in the United Arab Emirates, and 70 years in Kuwait, compared with 75 years in the industrial capitalist countries. Again, the adult literacy percentage is 25 in Saudi Arabia, 56 in UAE, and 60 in Kuwait, versus 99 in the developed countries.   This is not to say that oil wealth has brought no improvements in the standard of living of the mass of people in the Persian Gulf. To the contrary, the same social indicators we have cited to indicate the gap with the developed countries have shown substantial improvements from twenty years earlier. For example, the Saudi literacy rate is up from only 3 percent while life expectancy is twelve years greater. Hence, we would not disagree with the conclusion of Middle East expert Joe Stork that in the ten years after 1973

> the most basic material conditions of life improved for millions of people. . . . Within the oil producing states themselves, the dispersal of this wealth took the form of direct and indirect government sub-sidies and welfare programs, largely restricted to nationals and typi-cally affecting the poorest and richest strata. . . . The amelioration of material conditions for the lower classes, and the mobility and op-portunities for individual enrichment available to the better off classes, is one factor explaining the absence in the Arab world of any sustained class-based revolutionary movements or currents over the last ten years.

Missed Opportunities

At the same time there is considerable evidence that at least to date a great opportunity to generate rapid economic development relatively painlessly through oil wealth has been missed. The hope of economic planners and technocrats was that the historic pattern of economic development generated from an economic surplus initially produced by greater income inequalities could be avoided in the oil-producing countries. Since the economic sur-plus in these countries would be provided by nature rather than human suffering, the planners believed growth could take place side by side with increasing income equality.

Other experts hoped, even more idealistically, that the wealth generated in the Arab oil-producing countries could propel the whole Arab world upward. After all, why should the vagaries of boundary lines arbitrarily drawn by colonial powers combined with nature's random distribution of oil resources determine that population size be inversely correlated with oil wealth? Alas, on that score, there is overwhelming evidence of the failure of the dream. As R. Paul Shaw has pointed out, in the Arab world:

> That schisms in per capita incomes are wide between oil-rich and oil-poor countries is well known. . . . [In 1970] the absolute differ-ential . . . was only $460. . . . By 1980 it had swollen to over $5,000

per capita and the ratio of per capita incomes in oil-rich versus oil-poor countries had more than doubled to 7.3. . . .

Financial disparities are even more apparent between the two groups' countries when we consider differentials in the growth of accumulated wealth. Net foreign assets, for example, grew from a ratio of 8.74 in 1974 in favor of the oil-rich countries to over 31 in 1982.

Inequalities in the access to liquid disposable assets are hardly a sleeping giant. They are bulldozing a huge rift between oil-rich and oil-poor countries in the form of massive investments in social overhead capital. . . . [From 1976 through 1981] on a per capita basis, the oil-rich countries invested an average of $1,360 per year versus only $115 for their oil-poor counterparts.

Data like the above underlie the conclusion of Ghada Talhami that "the oil regimes' nationalist revolution against the international oil companies was not matched by an OPEC revolution of abundance in the entire Arab world." However, some economic planners may still argue that within individual oil-producing countries, a basis has been laid for future economic development that will greatly benefit all the people within the country, and perhaps ultimately the oil-poor countries in the region. To show that this too is an illusion, we want to now examine the behavior of the "rich" oil-exporting countries over the last decade in terms of its probable impact on future economic development prospects.

The Size of the Bonanza

From 1973 through 1982 all Arab oil-exporting countries together received oil revenues adding up to about $1 trillion. Of this amount, the rich Persian Gulf countries accounted for almost three-fourths, with Saudi Arabia alone receiving more than one-half, or over $500 billion. (To truly appreciate the revolution that OPEC has wrought since 1973, one must recognize that these Persian Gulf oil revenues had jumped on an annual basis by over twenty times the sums received in the 1970–1972 period.) The critical question in terms of possible future economic development in these rich countries is how was this enormous bonanza utilized?

Based on data for all seven OPEC countries, about 65 percent of oil revenues in the 1970–1982 period were used to pay for imports of goods and services, for both consumption and investment. Five percent was used for aid to other third-world countries. The remaining 30 percent has been used for foreign investment, primarily in the form of financial assets issued by Western banks, corporations, and governments. By the end of 1982, Saudi Arabia alone had accumulated net foreign assets (both private and governmental) of over $150 billion, or 85 percent of the total for all Arab OPEC countries.

From the vantage point of future economic development prospects, the hundreds of billions of dollars that have been piled up in Western financial assets represent a two-edged sword. An optimistic view would be that they are a kind of national "treasure chest" available to the country when needed. A more realistic view, in our opinion, would be that the future availability of these funds is severely limited by the fact that "the lion's share of petrodollar surpluses are held directly or indirectly through foreign branches of domestic banks in the United States and the United Kingdom."

As such, they are hostage to the United States and Great Britain. That this is not a mere metaphor can be seen from the fact that in 1980 the U.S. government "froze" about $8 billion in Iranian assets in the West, as part of the struggle over the Iranian seizure of U.S. embassy personnel as "hostages." Thus if, for example, a revolutionary regime were to take power in Saudi Arabia, it is highly questionable whether these financial assets would be available to it; at the least, control of these assets by the United States and Great Britain would give these countries great leverage over the policies of a new government.

Another less obvious factor that may make this money unavailable for future economic development is that a sizable, but unknown, share of the financial assets has been accumulated by private citizens of the oil-exporting countries. Normally these assets have been taken out of the country for reasons of security, often by people in and out of government who have made huge profits from various forms of illegal or quasi-illegal activity. As such, given changes in the home government in the direction of more honest practices, it is highly unlikely that the money would ever return home. This is a point to which we shall turn in more detail later.

As for the bulk of the petrodollar bonanza, which has been used for importing goods and services, there is little data available that would allow us to definitively categorize these expenditures in terms of their usefulness for development. As we noted earlier, some of the petrodollars clearly have been spent on useful investments in human and physical infrastructure, such as education, improved health, roads and communications, and so on. However, there is a great deal of impressionistic evidence to suggest that a very large part of these petrodollars have been used for wasteful luxury imports and expensive large-scale "development projects" that do not contribute to real economic development. Moreover, as we shall try to show now, this situation does not come about accidentally or because of errors of judgment, but is the very logical outgrowth of control of the state in most oil-exporting countries by small groups that harness the state for their own private profit.

Private Profits

Indeed, in our view, events in oil-exporting countries epitomize a tendency characteristic of third world countries where the state accumulates large amounts of capital, namely, the tendency for private groups to use their control of the state to transfer this capital to the private sector. This problem is potentially most crucial in the natural resources area, because in most third world countries the state either directly or indirectly accumulates capital in its role as ultimate resource owner or as tax collector.

The fundamental problem for the private sector is how it can obtain access to this state-controlled capital. In earlier times it was usually possible for the private sector to appropriate directly what it coveted. In the modern era, however, when even very underdeveloped countries tend to have significant technocratic forces operating within the state bureaucracy, this transfer problem is no longer so simply accomplished. (Although outright looting and corruption still occur, as the case of the Shah's Iran shows. There a list of government officials who were sending money abroad in the capital flight of early 1979 revealed near the head of the list the president of the National Iranian Oil Company, who had sent out tens of millions of dollars; this, of course, is small compared to the enormous wealth that the Shah and his family and associates accumulated and sent abroad.)

One way for the private sector to deal with this capital transfer problem is to be allowed to buy interests in the state sector. A good example is the recent Saudi activity in this direction, as trumpeted by the Saudis themselves: "The first flotation of shares in the state industrial holding company, Saudi Basic Industries Corporation (Sabic), has pointed a new direction for the public sector. Privatization of industry has emerged as a concept conducive to local business traditions which in the future will play a key role in government thinking."

However, where such a direct transfer to the private sector is not possible, as is often the case, another mechanism would seem to be even more important. This, ironically, is what may be called a process of "too rapid" economic development. Such a process can occur because in order for the capital accumulating in the state sector to be appropriated by the private sector, basically it is necessary for the state sector to spend this money (preferably within the country). Thus for the private sector to profit from the state's accumulation of natural resource wealth, it becomes necessary that various investment projects be started within the country, and the more the better. Thus only by having the government issue contracts for road construction, housing, airports, steel mills, and so on, can the indigenous private sector then share in the wealth (while even a little of this may trickle down to the lower sectors of society).

What this structural situation implies is that in countries with large revenues from oil and where there is private control of the state (either alone or, more usually, in cooperation with military and technocratic groups), investment of these oil revenues is likely *necessarily* to be wasteful and inefficient, from the viewpoint of society as a whole. Thus, the usual criticisms of these policies, along the lines that these *nouveaux riches* countries are wasting their resources by trying to spend far greater amounts of money than their economies have a capacity to absorb and hence money is wasted through inefficiency, inflation, and corruption, often miss the point.

Waste and Private Gain

The fact is, from the point of view of the indigenous private sector (as well as their collaborators at home and abroad who share in some of the "waste"), the more waste and inflation the better! By way of illustration, if a country has a labor force and physical plant capacity to absorb only $1 billion per year in investment at prevailing prices, and the government orders $3 billion worth of investment projects in a year, the natural result of market forces will be that those controlling the capital and the factors of production, that is, the private sector, will bid up their prices so that the full $3 billion is spent; the private sector will then absorb $2 billion in "excess profits." (Since some of this inflationary pressure could result in higher wages, to avoid this the private sector will seek either a large surplus labor force or a repressive apparatus to control the workers and/or their trade unions—conditions that prevail in many oil- and mineral-rich countries, not the least being the Persian Gulf oil exporters.)

This pressure to "invest" too rapidly is reinforced by the fact that the ruling elites in oil- and mineral-exporting countries frequently have a relatively short time horizon because they do not expect to be able to stay in power in the long run. Therefore they have even greater incentive to transfer the resources from the public sector to the private sector as rapidly as possible in order to get money while they can, and transfer much of it abroad for safety.

Indeed, inflation through this large and too-rapid project investment is a near-ideal mechanism for shifting accumulated capital from the public sector to the upper levels of the private sector. For one thing, there is no need for outright "corruption," since market forces will siphon off the profits to private capital in an apparently "normal" way. This is particularly important because of the existence in many third world countries of modern trained bureaucrats who will insist on "honesty" in government, and will struggle against and be in a position to expose outright corruption. Moreover, it is important for the efficiency of the state bureaucracies that corruption not be so widespread as to sap morale; again, too much outright corruption raises the danger of a coup within the country from anticorruption forces, particularly within the military.

Furthermore, the multinational companies of the industrial countries, working hand-in-hand with their international financial institutions, also have found these inflation-generating project mechanisms to be very useful. This is because such large projects, insofar as they involve contracts for foreigners, rechannel the flows of wealth from the resource-exporting countries back into the industrial countries (or more pertinently to the multinational companies controlled by these countries' own ruling elites). Thus, it is not surprising that the multinational companies, in such fields as engineering, construction, and provision of capital equipment for resource-exporting countries, themselves recapture a large part of the accumulated surplus.

Evidence for this in Saudi Arabia can be seen from the 1984 upturn in capital spending, in which "foreign contractors have reported a frenzy of bidding," and the Saudi government goal is to obtain a minimum share for local subcontractors of only 30 percent of the value of contracts; implicitly, foreign contractors have normally been obtaining more than 70 percent of the revenues from these huge government contracts.

Additionally, large-scale projects also harmonize nicely with the tendency of state bureaucracies to build bigger and bigger empires. By this mechanism they themselves obtain a larger share of the state's accumulated surplus (even if it is very small compared with the private sector's appropriation), through higher salaries, perquisites, and so on, and also gain greater power and prestige within the society. Thus, large-scale projects can be the unifying force between the indigenous private sector, the foreign private sector, and the state technocracies.

Government Support

By way of example, the following appeared recently in a *Wall Street Journal* advertisement, under the heading "Big Boost to Saudi Private Sector":

> A recent move to stimulate private sector investment in industry has been the royal decree setting up the National Industrialization Company (NIC). This company, capitalized at SR 600 million ($171 million), is to begin work by the end of 1984, helping to channel

local and foreign money into manufacturing. NIC's chairman is Mahsoun Jalal, a former director of the Saudi Basic Industries Corporation, the public sector industrial holding company, and ex-managing director of the Saudi Fund for Development which lends to Arab and developing countries.

"NIC will play a useful role in mobilizing investment for industry," says Jalal. "We are already studying about 30-40 projects. In each one that we back we will put in 30-40 percent of the capital. The rest will come from the private sector or from foreign joint venture partners."

In conclusion, in our view the tragedy of the oil-rich third world countries is that despite the great strides they have made in loosening the bonds of the international oil companies, their people are still prisoners—prisoners of a complex and subtle web of relationships between the forces of international capitalism and the ruling elites of their own countries. Although the long era when the international oil companies backed by Western economic and military power nakedly plundered the oil-rich countries is happily over, the wealth that oil produces is still being dissipated for the benefit primarily of foreign companies and small sectors of the local population. Thus, until governments come to power in the oil-exporting countries that are run for the primary benefit of the mass of the people, the potential of oil wealth will not be realized. Considering that oil is a nonrenewable resource, such changes must come sooner rather than later if that potential is ever to be realized.

6

On the Margins: The Developing Countries and the International Oil Industry

Although developing countries account for three-fourths of the world's population, taken together these countries still consume less than one-sixth of the oil used in the world (outside the Soviet Union and Eastern Europe). For the most part, the oil-importing developing countries have been treated by the international oil companies as minor irritants or, at best, minor sources of marginal profits or increased bargaining leverage in the oil companies' battles with major producing nations. Thus these countries have received only a small fraction of the exploration effort that has been lavished on the more developed countries in general, and the United States in particular. As late as 1981, for example, some 15,000 exploratory wildcat wells were drilled in the United States and another 3,000 in Canada, compared with 115 in all of Africa south of the Sahara, and only 1,000 in all of Latin America.

While the developing countries may be peripheral to the international oil companies and the home governments of those companies, from the point of view of the more than 2 billion people living in the third world, the energy crisis is far from peripheral. The situation of the oil-importing developing countries is even more dire than that of Western Europe and Japan. While the industrialized countries have the option of conserving energy, such conservation policies in developing countries would severely limit the possibilities for growth. Industrialization and modernization of the economy typically require an even faster rate of growth in energy consumption than the growth rate for the economy as a whole; only after the economy has matured is it usually possible to cut energy consumption growth rates without sacrificing living standards. Moreover, many of the developing countries lack adequate domestic energy resources; in some cases, such as the Caribbean, this is a result of the small size of the country plus geological bad fortune, while in other cases, notably West Africa, it is a result of a lack of adequate exploration in the past or the inability to mobilize finance and technology to exploit known energy reserves.

Another factor that increases the developing countries' problems with respect to energy supplies is their chronic shortage of foreign exchange. This shortage has been made vastly more severe in the past decade by sharply increased prices for imports from the industrial countries and for oil imports, as well as by the ever-increasing burden of debt incurred in order to finance these imports. In many countries by the early 1980s, one-half or more of all foreign exchange earnings was going to meet debt service payments, with most of the rest for energy imports, leaving virtually nothing for importing the capital goods necessary for modernization of the economy.

Foreign aid for energy, including subsidized loans through such agencies as the International Development Association (the World Bank's "soft loan" window), has filled only a small proportion of the foreign exchange gap. Moreover, much of Western aid is given by countries, such as the United States and Great Britain, or by international agencies dominated by those countries, such as the World Bank; in either case, the international oil companies are in a strong position to influence the pattern of aid giving. The effects of this influence can be clearly seen from even a cursory look at the history of the World Bank's role in financing petroleum projects in oil-importing developing countries.

As early as 1960, the World Bank commissioned and distributed to the governments of the developing countries a study prepared by leading oil consultant Walter Levy that strongly opposed active government participation in third world oil exploration and development. In a similar vein, the bank actively opposed the Indian government's plans in the early 1960s to undertake overseas oil exploration. In fact, until 1977, the bank never lent any money at all to developing countries for petroleum exploration and development.

More recently, the World Bank has shifted its policy and provided some funds for petroleum exploration and development, but in the context of an overall policy that still regards international oil company investment as the favored means of finding and producing oil. Even where these loans go to state oil companies, as, for example, in the case of India's borrowing to finance development of the Bombay High offshore oil fields, they have been linked to World Bank projects designed to increase private-sector investment in other oil projects.

Strategies of the Developing Countries

While most developing countries share these basic problems related to energy policy, they differ among themselves in both their objective conditions and the goals and strategies they pursue. Each government has to weigh a number of considerations, including: (a) the planned structure of the national economy; (b) the costs to the particular country of various foreign and domestic energy supplies; (c) the ability of the country to shift consumption from one energy source to another; (d) the ownership and control of energy resources and production—whether by the state, by local capitalists, or by foreign interests; and (e) the economic, political, and social impacts of different possible energy growth and utilization patterns.

Concerning overall development strategy, most developing countries have opted for relatively rapid industrial growth, with comparatively less emphasis on agriculture. Because energy requirements per unit of output are usually much higher in industry than in agriculture, this strategy usually implies a severe strain on energy supplies, which will have to grow more rapidly than the growth of the economy as a whole. A related issue is the approach taken to planning the economy's transportation system; a motor vehicle–based system (like that used in much of Africa, for example) requires huge supplies of petroleum, in contrast to a transportation strategy based on electrified or coal-burning railroad links (as, for example, in China or the Soviet Union).

Energy Costs

For an individual country the issue of the cost of energy needs to be approached from several different perspectives. First, there is the issue of whether energy supplies can be obtained domestically (local coal and wood, for example) or must be imported using scarce foreign exchange. Second, there is the issue of whether high initial capital costs (as for hydroelectric plants) or high operating costs (as for oil-burning diesel generators) impose more of a strain on a particular country; the answer to this may depend on the country's current debt load and its future export prospects. Third, there is the question of the social costs of energy supplies; what effect on the structure of society and politics does, for example, a decision to use imported oil and rely on the international oil companies have, as compared with a strategy of building up nationally owned energy sources relying on domestic deposits?

These cost factors must also be balanced against the flexibility of different energy sources. Nonoil energy sources are relatively limited in the different uses to which they can be put. Hydropower potential, for example, can only be converted to electricity for distribution through a grid system to fixed users, and coal is typically usable only in industrial plants, for railroads, and for small-scale home use. In contrast, oil and refined oil products have a high degree of flexibility; they can be used to produce electricity directly in industry, and as transportation fuels for all modes of travel. Thus, a shift from oil to other fuels, even if it saves a developing country foreign exchange, will often entail a loss of flexibility in economic planning.

Lack of ownership and control of energy enterprises can have serious consequences, as shown in the inability of developing countries to obtain their fair share of exploration effort from the international oil companies. As will be discussed below, a major effort of the third world in the past two decades has concerned national ownership; first to assert ownership of energy resources themselves (under the principle of "permanent sovereignty over natural resources"), and, second, to acquire ownership and control over actual energy exploration, development, and production efforts. While the first aspect of this drive for control has received wide acceptance, only a few oil-importing countries have made significant headway. Even in those countries where there are large, highly competent state oil companies, such as India, Brazil, and Argentina, these enterprises operate alongside the international oil majors and, if anything, face a more difficult task than the majors in raising capital in international financial markets.

Furthermore, strategies involving choices of energy resources almost invariably imply choices as to foreign versus domestic ownership as well. Few multinational companies, for example, are interested in investing in third world projects, such as coal or hydropower, that produce energy for internal use; the profits that the multinationals seek are available primarily through exports. Thus a country's decision to emphasize nonoil resources means that it will of necessity choose to operate without multinational corporation investment (with the exception of a few big export-oriented coal projects, such as those of Exxon in Colombia or Occidental in China).

Choices Among Energy Sources

Other considerations relevant to the developing countries in formulating energy strategies concern the potential by-products, both physical and social, of different energy sources. For example, a strategy that emphasizes the development of hydroelectric potential can also promote irrigated agriculture and flood control objectives. Similarly, development of petroleum, and especially of natural gas, can help to build up a petrochemical industry that might serve as a focal point for industrialization. (Petrochemicals, however, are likely to be less attractive as investments in the 1980s and 1990s, especially where domestic demand is small and a large part of the output must be exported, in view of the massive worldwide overcapacity in this industry.)

The scale of energy-supply projects is also an important consideration. In the immediate postwar period, the emphasis in many developing countries was on massive, capital-intensive developments, such as the large hydroelectric projects in Africa, Latin America, and Asia, often financed by the World Bank. Power from these dams was produced in such large amounts that it was necessary to find a few large-scale users to justify the investment; a typical example is Ghana's Volta River hydro project, which supplies power to the Kaiser-Reynolds aluminum smelter. But often no provisions were made to use any of the power from these large projects for rural development, and villagers near the dam could see the high-voltage power lines passing overhead while they themselves had no electricity at all. More recently, however, a number of countries, especially in South and Southeast Asia, have been emphasizing "mini" and "micro" hydropower developments, in which generators are simply placed in a river channel, without the need for building expensive dams. Such small projects are being used in China, for example, to supply power directly for rural use.

Where hydropower is not available, any government that wants to promote rural development may find it necessary to rely on petroleum, and in particular on diesel fuel for small-scale electricity generation in rural areas and on kerosene for lighting; the latter is especially important to a government concerned with improving literacy. Increasing efficiencies in solar power, however, hold out the possibility of providing a near ideal solution to this problem of providing widespread sources of small-scale (and nonpolluting) energy at relatively low cost.

While it might appear that most developing countries have a reasonably wide choice of energy strategies, limited primarily by their resource endowments, in fact most of these countries have chosen to build their energy economies on imported oil, particularly on imported oil that is supplied by the international petroleum companies. Even in 1980, after the oil price and supply shocks of the 1970s, the non-oil-producing developing countries relied on imported petroleum for more than two-thirds of their energy requirements. Few projections of energy demand showed this dependence on petroleum decreasing very much in the remainder of the century, at least if these countries were to make significant strides toward industrialization and the improvement of living standards for the mass of their people.

There are several reasons for this continuing dependence on petroleum and on the international oil companies. In many countries, alternative sources of energy, such as hydroelectric potential, simply do not exist. And in many cases, important hydropotential sources straddle national boundaries, making any agreement on their use difficult. Major examples of this problem include the use of the Indus River by Nepal, India, and Pakistan, and of the Brahmaputra by China, India, Bangladesh, and Nepal, as well as the Mekong River in Southeast Asia. Furthermore, other potential alternative energy sources, such as solar power, have not been perfected as rapidly as they might have been, because the research and development efforts have been concentrated in the industrial countries, where the oil companies have helped limit government funding.

A second difficulty is that, even where domestic resources such as coal are available, the international oil companies, supported by their home governments and often by the international banks, have been able to establish their position in these countries' markets by underselling domestic resources. As we have seen, imported oil displaced coal in Europe under the Marshall Plan, so it is not surprising that a similar result occurred in the developing countries, which were heavily dependent on foreign aid and had even less ability than did Europe to stand up to the oil companies and their home governments.

Oil Company Efforts

The oil companies and their home governments have also waged a major effort to keep developing countries out of the oil business. As noted earlier, the World Bank for a long time refused to lend any money for petroleum projects, and even today links its aid to an accommodating attitude to foreign oil investment on the part of the recipient country. Although the individual markets of the oil-importing countries of the third world are small, generally the oil companies have opposed these countries developing any substantial publicly owned oil-sector capacity, whether in production, refining, or marketing. In part, this opposition stems from the companies' desire to control product markets in developing countries, which are expected to increase their oil consumption faster, as they industrialize, than the already industrialized countries. Also, however, the oil companies' opposition stems from the supposed demonstration effect that successful nationally owned and managed oil enterprises might have in leading the third world as a whole away from its dependence on the oil companies.

To promote this dependence, the oil companies and their ideological supporters (such as Walter Levy) have argued that developing countries do not have the technical capability to undertake oil exploration and development, that these countries do not have the financial resources for exploration and development, and that they cannot afford to take the risks inherent in this business. As we shall see, while these arguments sometimes have a kernel of truth, they are highly misleading in that the conditions pointed to are posed as absolute barriers rather than relative handicaps; moreover, the arguments do not take account of the benefits that may be achieved by the country from overcoming the handicaps, or the costs of not taking action and leaving everything to the oil companies. Unfortunately, taken together these widely accepted arguments constitute a "mythology" that has severely hampered developing countries' efforts to establish oil independence.

Three Myths

The first myth is that of technical incapacity. This has been amply disproven by such countries as Algeria, India, and Mexico, all of which have demonstrated in recent years their ability to run large-scale oil industries using virtually 100 percent national workforces. In some cases, such as Mexico's recent offshore oil discoveries and India's discovery of the Bombay High field, they have found oil where the international oil companies had previously failed to find it. Moreover, even those countries without a long history in the oil industry can undertake exploration in much the same way that the oil companies themselves do it—by hiring specialized technical contractors. Exxon, Mobil, and the rest of the companies do not, in fact, do much of their own exploration work; they hire specialized contracting firms that will, for example, carry out seismic surveys, process the data from those surveys, drill wells, run tests on the wells, and build facilities for oilfield development and production. There are hundreds of such firms serving the petroleum industry and, if developing countries can pay for their services, many of these firms will work directly for state oil enterprises without going through the intermediary of the international oil companies.

The second myth used to deter third world oil activity is the myth of the prohibitively high cost of oil exploration and development. While it is true that the total cost of finding and developing a major petroleum field can easily run into the hundreds of millions of dollars, this cost is divisible into several parts, and a developing country may be able to finance each part of the cost from different sources. For example, the initial cost of seismic surveys, to define promising drilling targets, is usually only a few million dollars, and money for this activity is available from a variety of international aid sources, including the World Bank and such bilateral aid programs as those of Canada, Norway, and the Soviet Union. The next step, exploratory drilling, typically involves costs that may reach $20–40 million for a single exploration "play," involving several wells. This is the most difficult stage of the process for a developing country—especially one without established oil production—to finance, since the risks of failure are normally still high at this stage. Here the crucial question for each country is whether it can "afford" to lose the money that might be involved in an unsuccessful drilling program. The answer will vary from situation to situation, depending in part on the capital available to the government in any given country, but in every case the question of affordability should be weighed relative both to the benefits that would be gained from a successful government effort and also to the benefits forgone by letting the international oil companies make the decision—a decision that might lead to no action being taken.

Finally, the question of risk in exploration is often overstated by the oil companies. Most exploration programs involve a series of steps, each of which helps to define the likelihood of success and each of which offers the opportunity of stopping, and cutting off further spending, if results are not promising. In addition, in large countries, there may be a sufficient number of different exploration targets so that the country can be reasonably confident that at least one of them will be successful. This spreading of the risk over many different targets is, in fact, exactly what the oil companies themselves do.

High-Risk Areas

It is true, however, that there are certain areas in which exploration by developing countries themselves may carry unacceptable risks, given the potential costs and benefits. For example, where the only prospective areas are in very deep water or are located far from shore or far inland from centers of consumption, the economics of development may mean that only a very large field could be brought into production. These considerations affect the prospects for success in exploration in such countries as the Dominican Republic, Sri Lanka, and Tanzania, where most prospective areas are in very deep water, or in Mali, Uganda, Zaire, and Botswana, where prospective areas are far from points of consumption. Similarly, there are some countries in which substantial exploration has already been carried out, with little or no success, and where the exploration risk may in fact be relatively high.

An alternative strategy in such cases would be for several countries to join together in cooperative exploration efforts to share the risks. By multiplying the number of exploration plays in which each government would be involved, and reducing the amount that any single government would contribute to any single prospect, such cooperation could permit a group of third world countries to plan their exploration on the same rational basis used by the oil companies. Such a cooperative strategy would help countries to see that for decision-making purposes "risk" and "affordability" are not absolute concepts, but have to be looked at in relation to each other and to potential benefits. (For example, if each of five countries had one exploration prospect that would cost $20 million to explore and with a one in five chance of finding $200 million worth of oil, alone it might not be willing to take the risk since there would be failure four out of five times; if the countries pooled their efforts and explored all five prospects, on average they would have one success and each would end up with $40 million worth of oil for their $20 million investment.)

In sum, all three of the arguments used to limit developing countries' ability to undertake their own oil exploration and development can be seen as constituting a plausible but misleading mythology. This mythology serves to rationalize and perpetuate the continued dominance of the international oil companies, even in times when they have little interest in exploring for oil in new areas. And when the companies do agree to explore they frequently insist on contract terms that guarantee them huge profits if oil is found and give them virtually complete control over operations; thus even if exploration is successful, the country may end up depleted of its natural resources in exchange for grossly inadequate financial returns and without developing any capability to control or operate its oil industry.

Recent Changes

The situation of the developing countries vis-à-vis the oil companies has, it is true, improved somewhat from the immediate postwar period, when a leading oil expert, Paul Frankel, could comment:

> [The companies'] relationship to the miscellaneous oil-consuming countries outside of Western Europe was still in the Dark Ages, as it were . . . there was no competition at all except for that between the few established major oil companies, and this, commerce being what it is, resulted in the maintenance of price levels and profit margins that were considerably higher than they were elsewhere—even after allowing for the substantial cost of transport and handling incurred, coupled with the comparatively small turnover. It was said, not without some justification, that the poorer a country was, the higher were the prices it paid for its oil.

In the wake of the Organization of Petroleum Exporting Countries (OPEC) oil price increases of 1973–1974, there was widespread expectation, at least among developing countries, that this situation would be reversed, and that they would receive some kind of price break from the oil-exporting countries. These expectations have, however, been only minimally fulfilled. Generally, the OPEC countries have insisted that all customers, including third world customers, pay the OPEC price; assistance has been more in the form of liberalized credit terms (Venezuela and Mexico have a loan-subsidy scheme for oil-importing Caribbean countries) or in grants and loans from OPEC countries, or from such agencies as the OPEC Fund, to help the developing countries pay for oil.

Some changes over the past decade have included increasing public ownership of oil refineries and marketing systems in many developing countries, as the oil companies have sold their already-depreciated facilities to governments—though they have often retained lucrative management and technical assistance contracts to run the facilities that they formerly owned. The growth of state ownership in one or another phase of the oil industry is shown by the fact that, by 1983, more than 100 developing countries had established national oil companies. Whereas in 1973 oil refineries in more than half of the developing countries were wholly owned by the international oil companies, a decade later, such 100 percent foreign ownership could be found in fewer than one-fifth of all developing countries. A similar shift toward national ownership has occurred in marketing facilities, as state enterprises have taken over the former Big Seven service stations in such countries as Peru, Brazil, Argentina, and Ghana.

At the production stage, a number of state oil enterprises have emerged as major players in the world oil game. Petrobras of Brazil and the Oil and Natural Gas Commission of India, for example, not only carry out the bulk of exploration in their own countries, but have also entered into a number of contracts with other third world countries (for example, ONGC of India is exploring offshore Tanzania, while Petrobras is active in Angola). Other oil-importing developing countries where the state oil company is an active explorer and producer, and not merely a silent partner with foreign investors, include Argentina, Chile, Egypt, and Jamaica.

New Agreement Terms

Another major shift in favor of the developing countries since the early 1970s has been in the terms and conditions of exploration and production agreements between third world governments and the oil companies. As late as the end of the 1960s, the typical agreement provided, at best, for a royalty of perhaps 12.5 percent and a 50 percent income tax on the oil company's profits—that is, if the country's tax authorities could penetrate company accounting and determine what the profits really were. By the late 1970s, aided by OPEC's efforts, these terms had shifted dramatically in favor of developing countries, with the government's typical split from oil operations, through one or another combination of production sharing, ownership of equity, royalties, and taxation, often exceeding 80 percent of the total value of the oil produced. In the oil "glut" of the early 1980s, however, as most companies reduced their developing-country exploration budgets, this trend was slowed and, in some cases, even reversed. Even some well-informed and knowledgeable countries had difficulty, in 1983–1984, in finding oil companies that would offer much more than the traditional fifty-fifty deal.

But none of these advances in the 1970s overcame the basic problem for most developing countries—the difficulty of paying for imported oil and still having any funds left to invest in real industrial development or even to import such basic necessities as food. In 1980, oil-importing developing countries spent $50 billion on oil purchases (at an import level of 4.5 million barrels per day), and most projections show this figure steadily increasing through the end of this century. Coupled with the increasing financing costs of servicing the third world's massive debt (much of which was incurred to pay for oil), this import bill makes any real development virtually impossible.

The only practical solution for this impasse, for most developing countries, is a strategy that focuses on the use of indigenous energy resources, whether these are oil, natural gas, coal, hydropower, or such newly important sources as solar energy or alcohol production from sugarcane. As the experience of the past decade makes clear, with a decreasing willingness by the international oil companies to explore in the third world, even if high profits are promised, and with an ever-increasing and ever more unmanageable import bill for oil, most countries can only benefit from a domestically oriented energy strategy. The strategy of integration into the capitalist world oil economy has clearly failed, and self-sufficiency appears to be the only plausible candidate to succeed it.

7

Avoiding the Energy Crisis: Strategies of the Centrally Planned Economies

The energy crisis that rocked the capitalist world in the past decade left unscathed, and in the crucial cases actually improved the position of, the centrally planned countries. This is because the largest of them in population—the Soviet Union, China, and Vietnam—have generally pursued strategies that emphasized self-reliance and the development of domestic oil and energy resources. The Soviet Union is a long-established oil producer, China has been developing its oil industry since the 1950s, and Vietnam, while still importing almost all of its crude oil needs, has been actively exploring for oil. Thus, by examining the range of experience of these three differently situated countries we can draw some important lessons regarding energy strategy, particularly for developing countries.

The Soviet Union

The oil industry in Russia is almost as old as that in the United States; a substantial amount of production was developed at Baku on the Caspian Sea by the Nobel and Rothschild interests in the 1870s, and by the late 1880s the Russian production, exported to Western Europe, had ended the marketing monopoly of Rockefeller's Standard Oil. By the end of the nineteenth century, in fact,

Russia had moved ahead of the United States to become the world's largest oil producer. This ascendancy was short-lived, however; by the start of World War I, the United States—based on new production from the giant Spindletop field in Texas—had reestablished its position as the dominant oil supplier.

The Russian Revolution of 1917 provoked the first concerted action by Western governments and oil companies to protect their interests—a forerunner of such later actions as the Western oil blockade of Iran in 1951–1953, followed by the 1953 coup in that country. Almost immediately after the 1917 overthrow of the tsar, the new Soviet government nationalized the foreign-owned oil industry. For several years, the U.S., British, and Japanese governments attempted to defeat the Russian Revolution by sending armies in support of the White Russian opposition; British troops actually occupied parts of the oil-producing Caucasus in 1918–1919. When these military efforts failed, the companies—Standard, Royal Dutch/Shell, and the Nobel interests—agreed in 1922 to boycott the newly nationalized Soviet oil, an action once again foreshadowing later boycotts of those countries that had the temerity to assert their right to ownership of their own oil. While the boycott eventually failed, under the pressure of European shortages, it did mark one of the first instances of concerted action by the oil companies.

Following a drop in oil production as a result of the post-Revolution civil war and Western interference, Soviet oil output recovered steadily. Today, the Soviet Union, with production of more than 12 million barrels per day, is the world's leading source of petroleum. And the recent development of major natural gas deposits in Siberia, which will be used primarily to supply Western European markets, will make the USSR the world's leading gas producer as well during the 1980s.

Despite this high rate of oil production, however, the USSR has followed a more balanced energy strategy than have most of the Western countries, placing greater emphasis on coal. In 1950, for example, when the Western European countries, under pressure from the U.S. Marshall Plan strategy, were abandoning coal in favor of imported oil, the Soviet Union still relied on coal for roughly half of its energy needs. Even today, despite vastly increased oil and gas production, coal still accounts for more than one-third of energy consumption within the USSR.

The role of planning

Unlike many developing countries, of course, the USSR is a vast, resource-rich nation, and has been in a position to export rather than import energy. Even so, its success in meeting domestic energy needs from indigenous resources reflects the value of carefully planned development that links energy exploration and development to the building up of the country's overall industrial base. In contrast to the Western countries, and especially the United States, where the rise of oil has been linked to the growth of private automobile transportation, virtually all of the USSR's energy resources have been directed, through the planning process, to industry and public transportation. If the Soviet Union had used private automobiles to the same extent as the United States, it would have needed to produce 30 percent more oil, just to supply the cars, not to mention the additional energy that would have been needed for road construction and related activities. Thus, by emphasizing public transportation, and especially the development of long-distance railroads, as the primary means of moving goods and raw materials throughout the vast country, the USSR planners made it possible to build up a high degree of energy self-reliance.

Even today, Soviet passenger car production on a per capita basis is less than one-sixth that of the United States. But even this amount of automobile traffic may place a strain on Soviet oil resources. Western analysts have been predicting at least since the mid-1970s that Soviet oil production would reach a peak of about 12.5 million barrels per day in the mid-1980s and then decline, to be replaced by increased use of natural gas. While gas can be used easily in industry instead of oil, it is not a viable substitute as a transportation fuel. Thus, the relatively low Soviet automobile production may be a necessity.

Energy and Foreign Policy

In addition to its emphasis on domestic self-sufficiency, the Soviet Union is also noteworthy for the ways in which it has used energy as part of its overall foreign policy. Broadly, this policy can be divided into three stages in the post–World War II era: (1) an "aggressive" phase, emphasizing energy exports; (2) a renewed focus on meeting domestic needs; and (3) a revival of exports linked to obtaining technology and capital from Japan and Western Europe.

In the first phase, roughly from 1955–1961, Soviet oil exports increased from 8 million to 40 million tons per year. The export sales were made not only to Eastern Europe, but also to such capitalist countries as France, Sweden, Japan, and West Germany, and to developing countries, including Egypt, Cuba, and Brazil. Moreover, aside from oil sales, the USSR was also extremely active in providing both financial and technical aid to developing countries in the oil sector. This assistance, which included help in searching for indigenous oil sources and in building domestic refineries, directly threatened the interests of the international oil companies, which had until then maintained a near-monopoly in the third world. The fears of the oil companies were reflected in a widely circulated 1962 report by the National Petroleum Council, an industry trade group in the United States:

> The ultimate goal of the Soviet bloc is to expand its political control, destroy freedom, and communize the world, and it uses its monopoly of foreign trade to further these objectives. This, in short, is the problem for the free world when trading with the Soviet bloc. . . .
>
> Without a doubt, Soviet oil is the most important element in the Soviet politico-economic offensive in the Free World. The communists are using it to procure vital equipment and technology, to create political unrest and spread communism. It is a weapon with which they hope to destroy the private oil industry.
>
> The seriousness of the Soviet economic offensive requires a concerted effort by the leading countries of the Free World to restrict further imports of communist oil and the export of strategic materials to the Soviets.

Twenty years later, it might be noted, the Reagan administration in the United States expressed almost exactly the same ideas when it attempted to convince West European countries not to buy Soviet natural gas and attempted to bar the European subsidiaries of American companies from exporting high-technology equipment to the USSR for use in building the Yamal gas pipeline from Siberia to Europe. These attempts, however, were ultimately squashed by the Western European allies.

In 1962, however, when the United States had more power

within the NATO alliance, it succeeded in pushing through an embargo on exports of oil pipeline components to the USSR and had some success in reducing Soviet oil exports to Western Europe. In addition, through the efforts of the Western-dominated World Bank and the International Monetary Fund, a number of developing countries (most notably India) were persuaded not to enter into barter arrangements for Soviet oil.

Recent policies

Following this Western counterattack on oil issues, and following the Soviet-U.S. confrontation over Cuban-based missiles in 1962, the USSR became much less active in assisting developing countries. During the remainder of the 1960s, Soviet exports remained stagnant, and technical assistance projects were limited to a relatively small number of the Soviet Union's closest allies in the third world.

Beginning in the early 1970s, however, the Soviet strategy shifted once more, this time emphasizing both increased exports and the use of technology and capital from Japan and the West. In 1972, for example, the USSR signed a broad technical cooperation agreement with Occidental Petroleum of the United States, and at the same time established a presence in Iraq and Libya, providing technical assistance and agreeing to buy substantial volumes of those countries' oil output, even though the Soviet Union's own production was more than adequate for domestic needs. A further sign of the new approach was the beginning of discussions with Japan that ultimately led to the investment of billions of dollars by Japanese firms in development of the East Siberian oil and gas fields.

A major reason for the new approach to the West may have been the prospect of declining oil production if new, high-cost reserves could not be developed promptly. A 1977 Central Intelligence Agency report, which was widely cited by Western analysts attempting to explain Soviet oil policy, predicted that the USSR's production and exports would reach a peak by the early 1980s, then decline sharply as already-discovered fields were depleted. While Soviet concern about such a possible decline—combined with the willingness of Japanese and European governments to finance and assist Soviet energy development as a means of safeguarding their own supply position—may have been a partial reason for the renewed internationalism of the Soviet oil sector (along with a desire to earn hard currency from oil exports), it is noteworthy that the predicted plunge in production has not yet occurred; in 1983–1984, Soviet exports to the West in fact increased.

For the remainder of the 1980s, it appears that the Soviet Union will maintain its links with Western Europe and Japan, both as sources of foreign exchange and technology and as customers for oil exports. Soviet industry is rapidly converting to the use of natural gas for internal industry so as to free oil for export and for transportation use, but Eastern Europe may find it more difficult to obtain adequate oil supplies from the Soviet Union. Some of these countries, notably Rumania, have reacted to the possibility of reduced Soviet exports by undertaking their own exploration efforts in developing countries.

China

While Russia was one of the first major producers and exporters of oil, China was one of the world's first important oil importers. "Oil for the lamps of China" (i.e., kerosene) was the first Western product that China willingly imported, and by the 1880s, Standard Oil dominated the Chinese market, sending a quarter of its worldwide exports to China. With the development of a cheap kerosene lamp, oil products reached a mass market, and by the start of World War I, kerosene was China's third largest import, after opium and cotton.

Despite the size of the country, and despite the existence of sizable oil deposits, as late as the Communist victory in 1949 China had virtually no domestic oil production and no indigenous refineries; it was simply a captive market for the international oil companies' refined products. As part of the immediate aftermath of the Communist victory, the majors' marketing facilities—among the largest foreign investments in China—were nationalized.

Compared with the Soviet Union, however, China was only marginally dependent on oil. Virtually all of industrial and commercial energy needs as of 1949 were supplied by coal; oil production was only 1 percent of national energy output, and the kerosene imports, while large in dollar terms, because of China's huge population, were insignificant from an industrial-development perspective.

China, following the model of the Soviet Union, pursued an energy strategy in the 1950s and early 1960s that emphasized domestic self-sufficiency. As part of this strategy, some oil deposits were developed, with Soviet assistance, and oil production increased fifteenfold between 1952 and 1962. Even so, as late as 1960, oil still accounted for only 4 percent of China's total energy supplies, and China was still importing about 4 million tons a year of oil, or more than half of total consumption.

The Sino-Soviet split, which led to the abrupt withdrawal of the USSR's technical assistance and oil supplies after 1960, forced China to follow an even more self-reliant oil strategy. Oil production doubled from 1961 to 1966 and then quadrupled between 1966 and 1972, by which time China had become virtually self-sufficient in oil.

After increasing at a compound annual rate of more than 25 percent from 1949 to 1977, however, after 1978 China's oil output remained virtually constant, at about 2 million barrels per day, as existing onshore fields reached their peak production levels. China, with considerably less experience in oilfield development than the Soviet Union, has also turned to Japan and the West for new approaches, especially offshore development. In contrast to the Soviet Union, however, where deals were made mainly on a government-to-government basis, and where Japanese and Western technology was fitted in to an already-existing oil sector, China's apparent dependence on the international oil companies is much more extreme.

Inviting the companies in

China's shift from a self-reliance strategy began almost immediately after the death of Mao Tse-tung in 1976. Initially, arrangements were made with the Japanese government for offshore exploration in northern China (Japan was already China's largest oil export customer). Then beginning in 1978, the Chinese approached virtually all the major international oil companies, offering the possibility of exploration and production contracts similar to, and even more favorable (from the companies' point of view) than, those being offered by many developing countries. For several years China was the "hottest" new oil play around, as dozens of companies sent executives to Beijing for protracted negotiations and predicted that offshore China would prove to be the next Middle East. Ultimately, beginning in 1982, the Chinese awarded more than a dozen offshore contracts to consortia of oil companies, including British Petroleum, Exxon, Atlantic Richfield, and Elf/ERAP. While initial drilling in 1983–1984 failed to turn up any giant oil fields, there appear to have been sufficient modest-sized discoveries to make it likely that the companies' contract areas would become a source of some export production later in the 1980s.

One side-effect of the Chinese opening to Western oil companies has been a decided reduction in the interest of these same companies in exploration activity in other developing countries. By one estimate, the oil companies had spent more than $300 million in China by the end of 1983. This focus on China, taken together with the overall redirection of oil company activity toward their home countries or other politically "safe" areas helps explain what we saw in the last chapter—the lack of oil company interest in high-risk exploration in the non-oil-producing developing countries.

Vietnam

Vietnam is an example of how a relatively small and poor country has managed in recent years to develop a highly advantageous and sophisticated strategy for its potentially crucial energy sector: offshore oil. In our view, the Vietnamese example illustrates how a government with a real commitment to long-term economic development can cope relatively rapidly with this extremely technologically advanced industry. The key is to have a combination of necessary ingredients: honest government, the political will and popular support to take the longer view, and knowledge about the international oil industry.

The background to the situation was that the possibilities of large amounts of oil existing offshore in the southern part of Vietnam first became known during the height of the Vietnam war—indeed, the oil potential itself became a significant factor in the struggle in the United States over whether to continue or end the war. The starting point was in 1968–1970 when various seismic surveys sponsored by the United Nations, the U.S. government, and international oil companies indicated that the area offshore South Vietnam was highly promising (as was much of the Asian Pacific area). At the same time, the ability of Western capital to exploit this potential was seen clearly as hinging on the outcome of the then raging war. In the words of *Petroleum Engineer*:

> The projected work pace for all of Asian Pacific could turn out to be woefully conservative, depending on how long it takes to settle the war against the communists in Vietnam. If and when the U.S. wins its objectives there, oil exploration conceivably could be successful enough to turn that part of the world into another South Louisiana-Texas-type producing area. This would be one of the biggest booms in the industry's history. It all depends on the Vietnam war, how long it takes to get the job done and how well the job is done.

Moreover, the search for oil offshore South Vietnam became increasingly crucial to the Nixon administration's plan for withdrawing U.S. troops by "Vietnamization" of the war (popularly known as "Asians fighting Asians"), as well as the survival of the Saigon regime itself. For one thing, the U.S. government clearly saw that, in the words of a State Department official, "the economy is Thieu's Achilles' heel" and that as U.S. troop withdrawals pulled out the main prop from under the economy, only the offshore oil industry could provide the level of capital inflow needed to help keep it afloat. Furthermore, by giving the oil industry a direct stake in the outcome of the war, the Nixon administration hoped to gain crucial political support for the war from this key power bloc.

Thus, every effort was made to attract the companies. In late 1970 an oil law was passed in South Vietnam, modeled on a Thai law written with the assistance of Western oil consultant Walter Levy, which provided very favorable terms for foreign investors. As part of the U.S. government's strategy for backing this oil exploration, the Overseas Private Investment Corporation (OPIC) considered expanding its insurance program to cover such offshore investment by U.S. firms. Plans were made for issuing lease concessions to the many interested foreign companies by the middle of 1971.

Sources of resistance

Fortunately for the Vietnamese as well as the American people, two powerful historical forces helped to put a damper on these plans, which held out the dismal prospect of an indefinite continuation of the war. One was the continuing heroic resistance of the Vietnamese people to the corrupt Saigon regime and its U.S. backers, which made such oil investment a risky project, particularly since the clear position of the revolutionary forces was that they would not be bound by any contracts for such investment. The other force was the antiwar movement in the United States, which raised to a national political level the question: "Are our sons dying for offshore oil?"

With the assistance of a small group of progressive technical and political experts, the mass pressure generated by the antiwar movement—for example, ten thousand letters and cards on the issue were sent to the Senate Foreign Relations Committee in response to a campaign spearheaded by an antiwar group known as "Another Mother for Peace"—led to various congressional hearings and numerous newspaper and magazine articles. At least partly as a result of the ensuing debate and uproar, the Saigon regime postponed the lease sales "temporarily," which turned out to be for two crucial years. (As evidence of the peace movement's direct impact on the issue, OPIC decided not to insure such investment, and the influential *Oil and Gas Journal,* which originally favored oil investment in Vietnam, reversed itself, arguing that the bad name the issue was giving the industry was not worth it.)

By mid-1973, with the signing of the Paris peace treaty, when the Saigon regime was able to proceed with its leasing plans, it was far too late to save itself; this appears not to have been recognized by many of the oil companies (or perhaps they calculated it was worth the risk, and that in any event a new government would have to deal with them). In the next two years many large and small oil companies obtained concessions from the Saigon government and undertook exploration. The most important discoveries were by Shell Oil (U.S.) in late 1974 and Mobil in early 1975—indeed, Mobil was still drilling on its site on April 30, the day the war ended. Interestingly, one writer has speculated that this speeded up prospecting effort may have inadvertently hastened the end of the war:

> [Thieu] made a conscious attempt to strengthen support for his regime at home and abroad by playing up oil prospects. This may have backfired, however, for the discoveries by Shell and later Mobil during the fall of 1974 and early 1975 could well have helped to trigger the final North Vietnamese offensive against Saigon. Reviewing Hanoi's reaction to Saigon's evolving oil program, one is struck by a steadily growing note of impatience and an undercurrent of anxiety that oil discoveries might become a critical factor in determining the course of the Vietnam struggle.

In any event, by all accounts the Saigon regime collapsed far more rapidly than anyone expected, and the Vietnamese government suddenly found itself having to deal with a potentially crucial offshore oil sector at a time when it was totally unprepared, in terms of either knowledge or capital. Historically, the primary energy source for Vietnam has been coal, mined in the north. The Soviet Union had provided some assistance in the oil area since 1954 when North Vietnam was liberated from the French, undertaking surveys that indicated considerable oil potential by 1960, and later assisting in oil exploration that led to the discovery in 1975 of an onshore gas field. Nevertheless, neither the Soviet Union nor China, Vietnam's two main allies at the end of the war, appeared to have the technical capability for rapid and massive development of the offshore sector, even if Vietnam wanted to rely on them.

Postwar issues

Given the country's desperate need for capital and the highly promising nature of the offshore oil sector, there was great pressure on the government to explore and develop as rapidly as possible. The situation was further complicated by the existence of the Saigon regime's lease concessions to many companies, mostly American, which had paid bonuses to obtain the concessions and invested additional sums in exploration; these companies expected their "property rights" to be respected and to be allowed to continue working their concessions on essentially the same contractual terms. At the same time, the Vietnamese still had hopes of building good relations with the United States, which would allow large amounts of technology and capital to be invested in Vietnam (including the $3.2 billion that President Nixon had promised in 1973 on the signing of the peace treaty), and to build such a relationship they clearly could not alienate the powerful U.S. oil companies. On the other hand, the U.S. trade embargo placed on Vietnam at the end of the war prevented the companies from working the concessions or even the use of any U.S.-made oil technology in Vietnam.

It would take a book to chronicle the ebb and flow of Vietnamese oil events in the last decade, buffeted as they were by so many issues of higher political and economic strategy stemming in part from the complex relationships that have developed among the key countries operating in the area—Vietnam, China, the United States, and the Soviet Union. Aside from questions of space, however, it would be most useful here to focus on the key elements of Vietnam's oil strategy itself, rather than on the complex factors that may have motivated this behavior; for it is the strategy that may contain lessons for other developing countries.

In a nutshell, with the assistance of friendly oil experts, from an early point Vietnamese government officials were able to see through the mythology of the international oil industry that we discussed in the preceding chapter. In particular, they were able to understand conceptually that their progress in development of the offshore oil sector, although initially a risky business and one that ultimately required large amounts of capital and very advanced technology, was not at the mercy of the giant oil companies that had gotten a head start under the old Saigon regime—most specifically, the U.S. giants, Mobil, Shell, and Exxon. Thus, the Vietnamese government did not have to accept, as the Saigon regime did, contracts giving the oil companies a relatively large share of the profits and virtually complete control of the operations.

Strategy vis-à-vis oil companies

From a theoretical viewpoint, the liberating keys were the recognition that the big oil companies did not control the necessary technology, but that it could be purchased by anyone, and that to develop a successful offshore oil industry only a relatively small amount of risk capital was needed initially; once oil was found, the development capital could easily be borrowed. On a practical level, evidence for this latter point was found in the contemporary experience of India, which as we have seen was able, once offshore oil was found by the government in the Bombay High, to borrow massive amounts for development from commercial banks as well as the World Bank.

Given the fact that some successful exploration had already taken place, it was even more logical to undertake the dual strategy fashioned by the Vietnamese government. On the one hand, the most promising areas where some oil had already been found were reserved for the government to develop at its own risk. On the other hand, less promising prospective areas were given out for oil companies to explore at their risk, but only after an exhaustive search for the best possible candidates and arduous negotiations to fashion contracts favorable to the government. Here, the Vietnamese took the couple of years necessary to learn the practical realities of the international oil industry, partly by learning from friendly experts and countries, and partly by testing theories in the crucial area of contract negotiations.

Part of the Vietnamese strategy for finding suitable candidates was to focus on the state oil companies of Western Europe and Japan. This was because the main goal of these companies is to find oil for use in their home countries, and thus they would be willing to accept a lower rate of profit than would the big private companies; additionally, these state oil companies in general were not in the position of the large oil companies, which had many exploration contracts around the world that could be jeopardized by offering Vietnam an innovative and favorable contract. For this same reason, the Vietnamese also looked to smaller oil companies for a better possibility of good contracts.

The result of this strategy was that in 1978 the Vietnamese signed contracts with two state oil companies, Ente Nazionale Idrocarburi (ENI) of Italy and Deminex of West Germany, and a consortium of smaller private Canadian oil companies led by Bow Valley Industries Limited. Without doubt they were the most favorable contracts attained by the government of a non-oil-producing country in the history of the oil industry. The key element was that unlike the typical production sharing agreement of that time, and of now, where a company that found oil would *receive outright* a share of all oil produced, under the Vietnamese agreements the successful company would get only the *right to buy* part of the oil produced, at some discount from world market prices. Typically, the companies would get the right to buy up to 45 percent of any oil found at 7 to 10 percent below world market prices. In effect, this translates into a profit split for the Vietnamese government of 95 to 97 percent of the value of oil produced, compared with the 75 percent average split prevailing then and the 60 percent average under the old Saigon regime contracts.

Just how revolutionary and innovative these contracts were can be seen from the fact that the oil trade press gave virtually no coverage to them, or to their implications. Indeed, many leading oil consultants and experts seemed to be unaware of these contracts. Some who did know of them tended to downplay their significance by arguing that since some oil had been found offshore Vietnam, the highly favorable terms won by the government reflected simply the "fact" that there was very little risk for the companies in their oil exploration effort. Unfortunately for these "experts," however, experience showed that indeed there was a good deal of risk: the companies drilled twelve wells and spent almost $100 million without success, and all have abandoned their search.

While this failure was also unfortunate for Vietnam, the country still had the possibility of obtaining oil through the other prong of its dual strategy: the government effort to take the risk of exploration on the most promising areas. Originally this was to be done with financial and technical assistance from Norway, with the cost amounting to about $45 million and Norway to build an offshore exploration training center in Vietnam.

Norwegian aid

Unfortunately for the Vietnamese, this aid program appears to have been aborted by the growing Sino-Vietnamese conflict, which culminated in war in 1978. In our view one of the main motives of the Norwegian oil exploration assistance program, which has been extended to other countries in the third world, has been to help Norway get a foothold in developing countries as a supplier of oil technology and services. This is a sector that has grown rapidly in Norway through the development of North Sea oil, and the country clearly envisions that when this oil runs out the service sector will need to take up the slack, with the third world being the most promising area. Given this, with Vietnam and China clashing not only militarily but over boundary claims in offshore waters, and China clearly representing a far larger potential market for Norwegian oil services than Vietnam, it does not seem surprising that the Vietnam oil aid program was largely abandoned. Perhaps as reward for its favoring of China over Vietnam, Norway's state oil company, Statoil, was selected as the principal foreign advisor for China's oil exploration effort.

Ironically, the one component of the original package that was actually provided, the building and staffing of an offshore exploration training center, turned out to be a mixed blessing. This is because Norwegian technical assistance workers at the training center in Vung Tau joined with members of the three Western oil groups exploring offshore to smuggle an estimated $35 to $40 million in gold out of Vietnam, at a profit of about $12 million. The lengths to which these "aid" workers went in their moonlighting efforts is graphically described by the *Wall Street Journal:*

> Once they started, the Vung Tau community smuggled gold at a furious pace. A core of 20 to 30, including about 15 aid workers— half the Norwegian team—devised various means to smuggle the gold out of Vietnam: false-bottomed suitcases, stuffed in hollow ornaments, even gold-lined cosmetic cases so heavy they could be lifted only with difficulty by the wives who had to carry them. . . . a couple of Norwegians are thought to have made more than $1 million each.

Considering the small size of the aid program, the gold smuggling costs to Vietnam probably more than paid for this "assistance."

In any event, while the war with China and the unavailability of Norwegian technology and capital were undoubtedly setbacks for Vietnam, since then the Soviet Union has been able to step into the breach. In mid-1980 the two countries signed a comprehensive agreement for "cooperation in geological prospecting and extraction of oil and gas." In 1981 Vietsovpetro, a joint Soviet-Vietnamese petroleum development organization, was set up. Its first target area for exploration was the promising Bach Ho structure, where Mobil had discovered oil, and which as we have seen the Vietnamese government reserved for itself.

The current situation

At this point in time it is not clear how successful this effort will ultimately prove, although in mid-1984 there were reports of an initial Soviet find offshore Vietnam. Some have claimed that the inability of Vietnam to obtain U.S. technology is "a major contributing factor" in the failure thus far to find large amounts of oil. Perhaps more to the point, since the Bach Ho structure at least is in relatively shallow waters, may be the observation of a Western diplomat in Hanoi that "the significance of the U.S. oil find in Bach Ho in the dying days of the Vietnam War was exaggerated by American authorities to sustain flagging congressional support for the government of then South Vietnamese president Nguyen Van Thieu."

In any event, since at present the Soviet Union is providing much of Vietnam's oil needs on a deferred-payments basis, and oil found offshore Vietnam could be used to help repay this obligation, it is clear that both sides have a great incentive to succeed in the oil search. Toward this end, it is also clear that the Soviet Union is helping Vietnam to build a long-term capability to control and operate its entire oil industry, including its refineries and the present small-scale production onshore. In the words of Nguyen Hoa, Vietnam's director of the department of Oil and Natural Gas:

> The Soviet Union has also extended extremely valuable assistance in the training of the scientific and technical personnel for the Vietnamese oil industry. Hundreds of Vietnamese engineers and dozens of Vietnamese doctors in geology, geophysics and other branches of the oil industry have graduated from universities in Moscow, Baku and other places in the Soviet Union. A large number of Vietnamese oil workers have been trained at different Soviet vocational schools. Hundreds of Vietnamese engineers and workers have been sent annually for practice and research in the Soviet Union.

Lessons from the Centrally Planned Economies

In the final analysis, it is this development of an indigenous capability to operate all levels of a country's oil industry that is the necessary key to true energy independence. What the Vietnamese case illustrates then, at another level, is the stages through which government oil strategy ought to move. Initially what is necessary is to gain sufficient understanding of the industry, particularly at the crucial level of political economy, to develop a rational strategy for utilizing and contracting for foreign resources; this can be done in a one to three year period, with the assistance of experts from friendly countries and trusted consultants. For the intermediate period there is a need to be able to monitor and control as much as possible of the industry's operations; this capability should be reasonably well developed in the next few years, and could be provided by a combination of outside assistance and a relatively small number of technically qualified indigenous personnel. Finally, over the long run, a country needs to be able to operate the industry as fully as possible, using its own people as much as possible.

One of the advantages of a centrally planned economy is that it can undertake the necessary measures over the long run to build this self-sufficiency precisely because it is planned and does not rely on market forces—forces that as we have seen lead to technology and capital being concentrated in the industrial countries. The examples of the Soviet Union, China, and Vietnam, despite numerous differences, do have this important commonality. In our opinion, the historical record bears ample evidence that if these countries had not turned toward planning, they would have ended up in the typical plight of third world countries: either with no knowledge of their resources or with those resources, once discovered, ruthlessly and rapidly exploited with little benefit sticking to the country.

8

Conclusions:
Recent Trends and Future Prospects

At present, oil and gas continue their domination of the energy
picture in the capitalist world (and the Soviet Union)—a domination that was essentially achieved in the decade after World War II
when oil replaced coal as the leading fuel. By now, only in China
and Eastern Europe do petrofuels account for less than one-half of
total energy use, as compared with more than two-thirds in the
rest of the world, and even China seeks to raise oil's share of
domestic consumption, subject to its ability to find large supplies
of crude oil internally.

The continued dominance of petrofuels despite the huge price
increases of the last decade reflects a number of factors. First,
there have also been sizable increases in the prices of the main
competitive fuels, coal and nuclear power, although not to the
same extent. Second, oil still enjoys unique advantages in its virtual monopoly of the enormous market for transportation,
whether via automobiles and trucks, railroads, or airplanes.
Third, there is an enormous capital investment in the existing
pattern of energy consumption, and any changes are likely to take
place in an evolutionary rather than a revolutionary way; thus,
conservation of oil in the past decade generally occurred at the
margins, for example, by replacing worn-out capital equipment
such as automobiles with new fuel-economizing cars, rather than
by scrapping all existing cars. Fourth, and related, the general
stagnation in the world economy in the last decade has tended to
retard this conservation effect, since a buoyant economy is neces-

sary for large-scale capital investment and replacement. Finally, despite the hue and cry after 1973 that the world was running out of oil, except for unique periods of short-term shortages related to political upheavals, there have continued to be ample oil supplies.

For these reasons, we fully expect that petrofuels will continue to dominate the world energy picture in the future, through the end of the century at least. Although price predictions are always dangerous, it seems highly unlikely that oil prices will increase anywhere near the fourfold jump (in real terms) they took between 1970 and 1980; indeed, for what they are worth, most forecasts of future oil prices see little if any increase in real terms. Second, at present there are no major technological breakthroughs that appear likely to challenge the technical advantages of petrofuels, and any future breakthrough would take many years to substantially cut into the petrofuel lead. (Although solar power has made great strides in the past decade and is likely to continue to do so in the future, even an optimistic growth rate for solar of a doubling each year would still give it less than 10 percent of the world energy market by 2000.) Moreover, since in our view stagnation in the world economy is likely to continue for many years to come, this will slow the rate of energy substitution. Finally, since already proven reserves of oil would allow production for thirty years at current consumption rates, supply should prove no barrier to the continued domination of petrofuels.

We have also noted that the rise of oil has been mirrored by the decline of energy self-sufficiency for most countries. From a general position of internal energy balance thirty years ago, by now the percentage of total energy supplies derived from domestic sources for the industrial countries has fallen to less than 95 percent in the United States, 60 percent in Western Europe, and only a little more than 10 percent in Japan; in the oil-importing third world the comparable figure is about 50 percent. This vast increase in international trade in energy, particularly in oil but increasingly in natural gas, in conjunction with the failure of the members of the Organization of Petroleum Exporting Countries (OPEC) to gain control of petrofuel distribution as opposed to production implies that the international oil companies will continue to remain at the center of the world energy picture.

Company Control

As we saw in Chapter 2, the last decade has been marked by a weakening of the oil companies' control of the energy industry, followed by a gradual rebound in that control. The 1973 OPEC revolution gave rise to a historic process of virtually complete takeover from the companies of their century-long control of crude oil reserves, production, and prices. While this was of enormous positive significance to the OPEC countries, it proved to be a boon rather than a death blow to the international oil companies.

For one thing, as noted, the companies continue to retain domination of oil and gas refining, transportation, and distribution—in the last decade refinery capacity in OPEC countries increased more slowly than in the rest of the world and OPEC countries at present have less than 10 percent of world refinery capacity. In addition, the OPEC-triggered price increases greatly increased the companies' profits from their crude oil production in the West and in non-OPEC third world countries; although their per barrel profits in OPEC countries may now be similar to the $.50 to $1 they made a decade ago, in places like Alaska they have climbed as high as $10. In the light of this situation it is hardly surprising that the seven majors' total profits more than quadrupled from 1972 to 1983.

This enormous profitability of the international oil companies—the five U.S. majors alone had net income in 1983 of $10 billion, or 15 percent of the total for the top 500 U.S. industrial corporations—gave them the wherewithal to offset the inroads made by OPEC and extend their control over the energy industry. One direction they moved in was increasing their ownership of other energy resources, to the point where they now control 55 percent of U.S. coal and 35 percent of uranium, as well as a strong position in the emerging solar power area. Another was to increase their oil exploration and development investment in the West, particularly the United States, and in non-OPEC third world countries.

However, because in the early 1980s the cost of finding and producing crude oil in a safe area like the United States was relatively high, the biggest oil companies increasingly found it safer and cheaper to "buy oil in the ground," that is, acquire oil reserves by taking over other oil companies. The upshot was that in the 1980–1983 period $35 billion was spent by the largest oil companies to acquire other oil companies, including the virtually incestuous purchase in 1984 of one of the seven majors, Gulf Oil, by another of the seven, Standard of California.

The Future of the Oil Companies

Thus, the international oil companies have consolidated their power and position in recent years by a process of geographical retrenchment, expansion into non-petrofuel energy sources, and increasing concentration of capital. For how long and to what extent this process of concentration will continue is difficult to know, subject as it is in part to the vagaries of internal U.S. political developments. However, it would seem that to the extent that this increasing concentration has been financed by a combination of piled-up profits and new debt, it will relieve for a while the pressure that was building up in the largest companies to find profitable investment outlets for their accumulated capital. As part of this, there may well be a reduction in exploration expenditures by the largest companies, but barring a complete collapse of the world economy, inevitably the high profits of the big oil companies will tend to push them again on an expansionist path. At the same time, they need more than ever the high oil price umbrella set by OPEC to protect against a sharp drop in oil prices, which could bring the now further extended oil companies to financial ruin. In both of these endeavors, the oil companies will need the power and backing of their home governments and their international financial institutions, for, as ever in oil, the tanker follows the flag.

As we noted in Chapter 3, historically the home governments of the leading seven international oil companies have had important reasons for actively supporting their companies. These include the fact that the major oil companies represent vast concentrations of economic power, which carries with it great political power, and that the companies' drive for crude oil and profits all over the world furthers government goals of assuring reliable sources of oil while bolstering the balance of payments. Moreover, one key mechanism for activating this government support is the continual two-way flow of personnel between the oil companies and the sections of their home governments that impact most heavily on oil matters, such as the State and Interior departments in the United States; this two-way flow ensures both that government thinking will reflect oil-company thinking and that oil companies will be aware of government strategies.

The most important source of support provided by the home governments has been military power, whether actually exercised or used as a threat. The very fact that Anglo-American companies have dominated the oil industry in the twentieth century reflects largely Anglo-American military dominance, as evidenced by the two countries' being victors in both world wars; moreover, the shift in relative power from British to U.S. companies in the post–World War II era itself mirrors the war's impact on weakening British military (and economic) power and strengthening that of the United States. Even in recent years, when the rise of the Soviet Union as an equally formidable nuclear superpower has made military intervention by the United States in oil-producing countries extremely dangerous, the use of force is still a major element of U.S. strategic thinking. The most important example is the continual threats, both openly and behind the scenes, by the United States since the OPEC revolution to intervene militarily in the Persian Gulf if U.S. oil interests are "jeopardized." Enunciated by both strategic planners and presidents, and backed by the Rapid Deployment Force, this belligerent stance is strong evidence of both the power of U.S. oil companies and the significance of oil as perceived by the U.S. government.

Limits on Government Power

However, because the nuclear era has made military intervention more dangerous (and because of the anti-interventionist backlash in the United States stemming from its defeat in the Vietnam war), its use for advancement of oil interests is likely to be reserved for the most vital cases. Thus on a general scale, the most important mechanisms of government support for the oil companies are likely to come from a combination of economic and political pressures. As we have seen, some of these are unilateral measures, the most notable in the United States being the revival of the Overseas Private Investment Corporation (OPIC) role in support of U.S. foreign oil investment. By providing U.S. companies insurance against "expropriation," and by then defining that term to include not just wholesale takeover but any "material unilateral change" by a government in the profit-split from oil production, OPIC has provided U.S. companies with a powerful weapon. This is particularly true because if OPIC decides that such a contractual violation has been made by a third world government, it can intervene by paying off the company and taking over its claim, and then turn the matter into an international dispute for which OPIC can call on assistance from international organizations such as the International Monetary Fund (IMF) and the World Bank.

This example illustrates another key trend in a nuclear era and one that is also marked by revived economic power for the non-Anglo-American industrial countries, particularly Germany, France, and Japan. This is the tendency to use multilateral financial institutions as a key mechanism for promoting Western oil interests. The advantages of using such international institutions instead of national ones is that they can reduce potentially damaging rivalries among the industrial countries while providing a kind of "fig-leaf" of international cooperation to veil the continuing attempts to exploit third world countries. The disadvantages are that since the goals of the Anglo-American oil companies and their home governments are still the same, allowing the ball to be carried by international institutions in which their industrial country rivals have a strong voice may be giving up too much.

The problem is shown in the struggle among the industrial countries and between oil companies over the most important mechanism that has been developed in the last decade to promote Western oil interests, namely, the World Bank's large-scale lending program to third world governments for oil exploration and development in their countries. This program is in part a response to the generally perceived need by Western governments to undercut OPEC's power by increasing future oil availability from non-OPEC third world countries, while at the same time preventing a scramble among individual industrial countries for access to third world oil supplies that could strengthen the bargaining position of these underdeveloped countries (OPEC and non-OPEC alike).

Whither the World Bank?

The ongoing struggle over the exact role the World Bank should play with this new lending program developed because since its inception the bank's primary role has been to lend money to third world governments to build infrastructures such as roads, power stations, and so on, that would lay the basis for foreign private investment to enter into the profit-making sectors. Given that overriding goal of this international institution, which is financed and controlled by Western economic interests, historically the highly profitable oil exploration and production sector was the private terrain of the international oil companies and off-limits for World Bank loans—indeed, the bank even used its power to try and block third world governments such as India from putting up their own capital in this area. Thus, it is a somewhat revolutionary idea for the bank to now help finance government exploration and development.

World Bank officials were quick to point out that in some ways the program was not as revolutionary as it appears, since the principal thrust was to tie the third world governments to partnerships with the international oil companies in exploring for oil, and on contractual terms that were about normal for the industry—in this way it was hoped that governments would be deterred from exploring for oil on their own. Nevertheless, Exxon in particular, as befits its position as the strongest and most widely diversified international oil company, lobbied strenuously within the U.S. government against the bank's change of position. And, thanks to this company's great political power as well as the almost religiously pro–private enterprise ideology of the Reagan administration, after 1980 the U.S. government did an about-face and worked hard to limit the bank's oil loans to third world governments.

Governments' New Role

Looking ahead to the possible future shape of the Anglo-American oil companies' relations with their home governments, we offer a few speculations based on recent trends. To the extent that the largest British companies have been interwoven with U.S. oil interests—particularly by British Petroleum's control of Standard of Ohio with its Alaskan bonanza and Royal Dutch/Shell's takeover of U.S. Shell—Anglo-American unity and power may be enhanced (especially for the period that the Reagan and Thatcher governments, which are ideological twins, remain in office). Additionally, to the extent that Anglo-American oil companies increasingly look to the West and away from OPEC for oil supplies, they will want OPEC production kept down in order to keep oil prices up. That Great Britain perceives it to be in its interests to maintain oil prices was demonstrated in 1983, when the actions of the British National Oil Company in keeping North Sea crude oil prices up was instrumental in preventing the OPEC price cut from $34 per barrel to $29 from going any lower. Thus, Anglo-American military, economic, and political power is likely to continue to be focused on the OPEC countries, particularly in the Persian Gulf, whether there is a surplus or a shortage of oil. All in all, this drive of Anglo-American oil companies and their home governments to maintain relatively high prices for oil is likely to bring them into increasing confrontation with their rival industrial countries.

As discussed in Chapter 4, in contrast to the United States and Great Britain, the major countries of Continental Europe and Japan were either defeated militarily in global clashes with the former or emerged with greatly weakened economies. Thus, they are the losers in the international oil struggle. Only France, which was on the winning side in the two world wars, was able to gain a foothold vis-à-vis the Anglo-American monopoly, and even its companies still supply less than 60 percent of French oil consumption. The oil companies of the former Axis powers of World War II have done even worse, with their production accounting for the following shares of home consumption: Germany, less than one-tenth; Italy, about one-sixth; and Japan a minuscule fraction.

International Energy Agency

Since 1973 the countries of continental Europe and Japan have tried to assure their future oil supplies by a combination of investments in and bilateral trade deals with OPEC countries as well as other potential oil-producing third world countries. At the same time, in order to try and protect themselves against a future cut-off of oil supplies, particularly from the Persian Gulf, these industrial countries took the lead in setting up after 1973 the International Energy Agency (IEA). The principal purpose of the IEA is to allocate oil supplies in the event of an emergency situation so that shortfalls of oil will be relatively equitably distributed among the Western countries, and they will not get into competition with each other that might cause the price of oil to skyrocket again.

At present the issue of the efficacy of the IEA is moot, since there is an oversupply of oil on world markets. Moreover, many countries have built up their own stockpiles in case of an emergency. Nevertheless, as events of recent years have dramatically demonstrated, crises can arise virtually overnight that could provide a severe challenge to the IEA "safety net."

In our opinion, given the long history of general economic and oil-centered rivalry among the industrial powers, the IEA is a frail reed to protect the individual countries. It is quite possible that if the emergency is of a short duration, then the system will work, because it will call for little real sacrifice. If, however, the emergency becomes prolonged and the "have" countries, particularly the United States and Great Britain, would be required to make real sacrifices in sharing the burden with the "have-nots" of Continental Europe and Japan, we are dubious that they would do so—at least without extorting enormous economic and financial concessions. After all, despite the rhetoric, when push comes to shove the motto of the capitalist system is still the cry of the elephant as he danced among the chickens: "Every man for himself."

Thus, in the event of a prolonged oil crisis, we would expect that the industrial countries would resort to more individualistic actions to protect themselves. This is not to say that there would not be some cooperation. For example, France, which at present is the only one of the oil-weak industrial countries able to project military power abroad, might well do this in conjunction with

Anglo-American forces. But, in general, we would expect Western Europe and Japan to utilize the various bilateral relations they have built up with oil-exporting countries for their own individual benefit. (For example, in spite of continuous fighting between Iraq and Iran, Japan has continued to push ahead with the construction of an enormous petrochemical plant in Iran that is likely to be a "white elephant"; at least part of the Japanese motive is to maintain good relations with Iran, which in normal times supplied a large part of Japan's needs.) To better understand these potential bilateral relations, however, we need to take a look at the present position of the oil-exporting countries.

As we saw in Chapter 5, although a relative handful of countries produce the bulk of the oil moving in international trade, this is not a new phenomenon—only the names of the exporters have changed. Again, history repeats itself in that just as global wars have played a crucial role in shifting third world oil assets among competing Western imperialist powers, a smaller regional war in the Middle East in 1973 played a key role in weakening Western control of the oil industry. The Arab-Israeli war and the oil embargo laid the groundwork for OPEC to seize control of prices and ultimately production and thus to increase greatly its share of oil profits.

OPEC's Position

In reaction to the subsequent world economic crisis and the reduction in oil demand caused by that crisis and conservation efforts, the international oil companies have taken measures that have weakened OPEC's power. Most importantly, they have shifted new investment for crude oil exploration and production out of the OPEC countries, both to the industrial countries and to third world countries. Basically, the companies were able to do this because OPEC countries controlled relatively little refinery capacity, so that unlike the companies they did not have captive outlets for their crude oil production. (In the 1980s, however, some OPEC countries are building a substantial amount of refinery capacity at home and buying existing refining and marketing facilities abroad, especially in Western Europe.) Finally,

OPEC power has also been weakened by the pile-up of its oil surplus in Western financial assets, which effectively serve as hostages against militant OPEC action—indeed, Saudi Arabian pronouncements about oil prices seem more concerned with protecting the value of the U.S. dollar than the unity of OPEC or the price of its oil.

Perhaps most importantly for the people of the OPEC countries, the leap in oil wealth since 1973 has failed to transform these countries (or their regions) in the positive ways that some thought possible. This is basically because these countries are controlled by conservative elite forces who work hand-in-hand with multinational companies and Western governments to siphon off the oil surplus for their own private benefit. Thus, those who control the state seek to shift assets to the private sector, which then transforms them abroad—either for luxury imports, or in investment deals with multinationals, or in Swiss bank accounts for security. In short, by and large the elites are more concerned with private looting than with societal development.

As for the oil-exporting countries' future prospects, based on recent trends they do not seem very promising. In our view, continued stagnation in the world economy, and oil and energy conservation, will serve to keep demand from growing very much. At the same time, the thrust of the international oil companies will be to look for new oil supplies outside of the OPEC countries and thus help undermine their power. And, insofar as conservative forces maintain their control of most OPEC states, little will be done to promote genuine economic development.

However, it would be a mistake to take too static a view of future prospects, particularly with regard to political stability in OPEC countries. Who would have dreamed in 1969 that four short years would see not only a tenfold increase in oil prices but the undermining of Western ownership and control of third world oil supplies that had been built up by two world wars and seven decades of imperialist exploitation? Or that ten years later a revolution in Iran would lead to a doubling of oil prices and involve the overthrow of the seemingly overwhelmingly powerful twenty-five-year police state of the Shah and his Western backers?

Thus when we admit, as we must, the possibility if not likelihood in the rest of the twentieth century of severe shocks to the world economy, the international oil industry, and the oil-exporting countries, then prediction becomes much more difficult. On the other hand, what we have learned from the history of this century is the enormous durability of the international capitalist system, and its leading components of international oil companies, in the face of tremendous upheavals. To the extent that in recent years this system has become more and more pervasive, penetrating into areas and countries that in earlier years were relatively isolated from it, it is more difficult for individual countries to break out of the system's control. A very good illustration of this is the predicament of today's oil-importing third world countries.

Oil-Importing Countries

As we saw in Chapter 6, historically and at present these impoverished countries have been of only marginal interest to the international oil companies. While the companies could obtain super-high per barrel profits on their sales of crude oil and refined products in these areas, since the principal markets for large volumes of oil were in the industrial countries, the greatest mass of profits came from exploitation of the oil-exporting countries. Thus there was relatively little exploration in the oil-importing third world, despite the fact that these countries comprised the great bulk of the world's land mass.

On the other hand, in the post–World War II period oil has been of sizable and growing significance to oil-importing developing countries. This has been most obvious in the area of foreign exchange, where the lack of indigenous oil places a serious burden on the balance of payments. Thus, even at the end of the 1960s when oil prices were at historic lows, for important countries like Argentina, Brazil, Egypt, and India, the cost of oil imports accounted for anywhere between 6 and 17 percent of the total import bill. By now, with the post-1973 tenfold increase in oil prices, for many developing countries oil imports make up half or more of all imports, leaving little room for importing other materials and equipment necessary for economic development.

Even in the earlier period of the 1960s, despite the relatively small volume of profits made by the companies from the oil-importing third world, the companies and their Western supporters still went to great lengths to maintain control of the oil industry in these countries. One reason was that since these countries had very large populations in total and were just beginning to industrialize, they were believed to be the areas with the most future growth potential for oil sales. Another reason was that the companies and Western interests were afraid that if the governments in oil-importing countries took control of the industry, this might have a very dangerous "demonstration effect" on governments in the crucial oil-exporting countries. The Western drive to maintain control over the oil industry in the third world was epitomized by the continuing efforts of the World Bank to block governments of developing countries from entering the industry.

In recent years, as we have seen, the World Bank has encouraged some participation by governments of oil-importing countries, but generally in conjunction with international oil companies. Thus, the bank continues to promote the mythology of the industry: that only the companies have the necessary technology and capital to be able to afford the risk of oil exploration and development. As we have argued, this is a mythology in the sense that while there is a kernel of truth in it that makes it plausible, in fact there are sufficient falsehoods in it that it should not prove a barrier to most developing countries undertaking oil exploration and development.

State Oil Companies

In the 1970s the success of a number of state oil companies in oil-importing developing countries has demonstrated in practice the essential falsehood of the mythology. Building on its long tradition of operating a wholly integrated oil industry within the country, Pemex of Mexico has been so successful as to turn the country into a major oil exporter. At the same time, the national oil companies of Brazil and India have been able not only to carry out the bulk of oil exploration within their own countries, but to undertake oil exploration abroad in other third world countries.

During these years many developing countries also took control of refining and marketing operations within their borders. At the same time, thanks to the changes generated by OPEC, developing countries in general were able to obtain much better contracts from oil companies for carrying out oil exploration and development. However, in the 1980s some of the ground gained has been lost. This is essentially because the combination of a prolonged recession for third world countries and the relative glut in world oil supplies has shifted the locus of bargaining power back toward the companies: the governments have less foreign exchange to undertake oil exploration and the companies need the countries less than before.

Overall, the difficulties the oil-importing developing countries are facing from the oil sector have and will continue to have a profound effect on their whole economies. Unfortunately, as in Europe and Japan, in the postwar period oil became the dominant fuel in most of these countries, even where large indigenous supplies of coal and/or hydropower existed. One might say that with the international oil companies and their Western backers acting as "pushers," these countries became "hooked" on the narcotic of cheap crude oil. This was accompanied by the development of industrial structures oriented to oil as the primary fuel, as well as middle-class consumption patterns with the same bias. The most notable example is Brazil, where the whole development strategy for decades was based on an "automobilization" premised on cheap (imported) oil; the jump in oil prices in the 1970s has been a major factor in turning the "miracle" into a debacle. But the developing countries in general are suffering all the pangs of addicts who cannot really afford their habit anymore.

Is there any way out of this tragic situation for the third world? In our view, given the likelihood that the international economic crisis will continue for a very long period, there does not appear to be much basis for optimism. One important step would be for each country to make a maximum effort to control and accelerate the oil-exploration effort for its own benefit—after all, for many countries even a small find would be of great value, while the international oil companies might be uninterested in pursuing anything but large finds.

On a more general level, we believe that third world countries have to make a maximum effort to remove themselves as much as possible from the foundering international economic system. This would require a restructuring of their economies to reorient them from production for export to production for local needs, utilizing to the utmost local labor and raw materials. In the energy sector, this would mean focusing not only on oil but also on potential small-scale energy sources, such as rural dams, solar power, and biomass. (If a number of third world countries begin to move in this direction, then one can envisage the beginnings of really meaningful trade relations and cooperation among them, not least in the energy area.)

The Centrally Planned Economies

What can potentially be accomplished by such a "do-it-yourself" approach is suggested by the historical experience of the centrally planned economies examined in Chapter 7. While after the 1917 revolution the new Soviet government inherited a long tradition of sizable crude oil production, this had been essentially controlled by Western interests. The subsequent Civil War and Western invasions, partly aimed at regaining these valuable properties, created chaos in the country, which sharply reduced production. After that, however, based on indigenous resources and personnel, the Soviet Union has painstakingly built up an enormous oil industry such that, despite the setbacks from World War II, it is now by far the world's leading oil producer, with output 50 percent greater than that of the United States.

At the same time, what is most significant about the Soviet Union is that as a planned economy it was able to shape the structure of its industry and transport and consumption goods to fit the availability and development of indigenous resources. Thus, for many years it relied heavily on domestic coal as the principal energy source, even while as we have seen Western Europe and Japan and much of the third world were becoming dependent on imported oil. This self-sufficiency could only have been achieved in a country where the government had the power to allocate resources and restrain the growth of oil-consuming sectors, most notably, private automobiles: had the Soviet Union achieved the same level of automobilization as the United States, for example, its increased oil needs would turn it from a major oil exporter to an importer.

The Soviet ability to expand oil production and limit consumption has given it an oil surplus, which generates much of the foreign exchange needed for vital capital-equipment imports. Historically, some of this excess oil as well as the know-how and capital equipment that the country has built up in the oil sector has been used as an adjunct of foreign policy, particularly in trying to win influence and assist friendly forces in third world countries. (This is an example that some oil-exporting countries have also followed, most notably Algeria with know-how and Libya with oil and capital.)

While many third world countries were assisted in developing local oil industries by the Soviet Union, the most important case is that of China. After the 1949 revolution, the new government, which inherited an economy almost totally reliant on coal but imported expensive quantities of kerosene, basically followed the Soviet model of emphasizing domestic self-sufficiency. Although with Soviet assistance the tiny level of domestic oil production increased rapidly in the 1950s, by the time of the Sino-Soviet split in 1960 oil still accounted for less than 5 percent of total energy consumption (while the bulk of that oil was still imported).

The rupture caused China to follow an even more self-reliant path. In oil this was particularly successful (indeed, development of the Taiching oil field became the heralded model for all industry), and between 1961 and 1977 oil production increased 1800 percent with China becoming a significant exporter, particularly to Japan. However, after the death of Mao in 1976, with China's oil production peaking in the late 1970s, the government shifted away from the self-reliant strategy and looked to the West for assistance. As part of the post-Mao drive for maximum-speed economic development, in which increasing oil exports were seen as the key to earning large amounts of foreign exchange, the country threw its offshore areas open to the bids of foreign oil companies.

In doing so, especially in a period of relative oil glut, China was forced to offer terms that were often more favorable to the companies than they could get in other developing countries. Thus, an important lesson for other third world countries from China's recent experience is that if a country wants to move very rapidly and on a large scale in the oil-exploration area in conjunction with foreign companies, it will have to give away a lot in future profits to these companies. Put simply, the faster a government wants to go, and the more the world knows that it is under pressure to move fast, the weaker is its bargaining power.

The main lesson of the Vietnam experience is the corollary: if you go slow, and if the world knows you are prepared to go slow, the greater is your bargaining power and the less you will be forced to give away. Like the revolutionary victors in Russia and China, the Vietnamese government inherited after the end of the war in 1975 a potentially crucial oil sector it was totally unprepared to exploit. While some oil had been found offshore South Vietnam during the war, the unexpectedly rapid conclusion of the war found the government completely lacking in the capital or technical expertise to explore and develop these finds. Moreover, there was great internal pressure on the government to have the offshore area exploited as rapidly as possible, in order to obtain capital for rebuilding the wartorn economy. Since at this point neither the Soviet Union nor China was in a position to supply the necessary technology for this very advanced area, it was widely believed that the Vietnamese would be forced to turn to the international oil companies—particularly the ones that had obtained concessions in the war period from the Saigon regime and were now clamoring for the right to continue working on these concessions (at the same highly favorable terms).

The saving grace for the Vietnamese was their strong political commitment to obtaining the maximum long-run benefits for their country from these nonrenewable resources; a history of literally thousands of years of fighting against foreign aggressors had imbued many Vietnamese with a uniquely "long view." As a result, despite the pressures, the government took the time to study the international oil industry, both on a theoretical level and in practice, and thus was able to overcome the mythology of the industry as it related to their own situation.

In particular, the Vietnamese were able to see, first, that the required oil technology could be purchased (despite an American embargo that at times made for difficulties) and, second, that only relatively small amounts of capital were needed for a limited oil-exploration effort. Given that oil had already been found in a couple of places, this also meant that the risk of a highly selective exploration effort would be minimal. Out of this analysis of the Vietnamese reality a dual strategy was developed and carried out.

The essence of the strategy was that the most promising areas,

assiste

where oil had already been found, would be reserved for the government to explore, utilizing technology and capital provided by friendly governments, while less promising but still attractive areas would be let out to foreign companies to explore; these approaches were to be pursued in parallel, thus speeding up the development of any oil resources and at the same time increasing the government's bargaining power with potential foreign collaborators.

Negotiating Strategies

Even where the government let foreign companies in, it did so only after taking the time to negotiate with many possible groups, playing one off against another in order to obtain the best possible terms for the country. In fact, Vietnam was able to achieve spectacular results by capitalizing on the oil-scarcity mentality of the late 1970s and targeting the state oil companies of Western Europe, which were anxious to obtain diversified supplies of crude oil for their home countries. Using the principle that the companies if successful would receive the right to buy part of any oil found at a discount off market price (rather than the prevailing principle that companies would receive outright part of any oil found), the Vietnamese obtained by far the best contracts of any third world government.

On the other front, the effort to explore the most favorable areas with Norwegian government assistance was delayed in the latter part of the 1970s by the conflict with China. With the Norwegians apparently more interested in pursuing their China connection, the Vietnamese turned to the Soviet Union. By the early 1980s the Soviets were in a better technical position to carry out offshore oil exploration, and while this effort has just begun and it is too soon to predict results, there have been reports in mid-1984 of at least one oil discovery.

Finally, having surveyed the long and complex history of the international oil industry, if there is one overriding conclusion we would like to leave with the reader it is the following. The continuing struggles among the major forces in the international energy industry have been played out against the backdrop of and in interaction with the global forces of the international capitalist system. And since in our opinion this system has entered on a period of prolonged stagnation and crisis, we believe the future of the oil industry is likely to be marked by heightened conflict. This seems virtually inevitable when the normal dog-eat-dog struggle becomes one not just for increased prosperity but for survival itself.

In this gloomy prognosis there is one ray of light. Conflict is a two-edged sword, and perhaps from it will emerge new forces, on an individual-country basis or on a global scale, that will help to free us from the tyranny of the international market system. For in a nuclear age, if we are to survive this century, let alone the next millennium, it is clear that competitive economic warfare will have to be replaced by cooperative efforts for welfare—not least in the international energy arena. One can only hope that this change will come sooner rather than later.

Appendix: Tables

Table 1.1
World Primary Energy Consumption
(million metric tons oil equivalent)

	1972	1982	% Annual Growth
United States	1,767.8	1,728.4	−0.2
Canada	179.7	207.4	1.5
Total N. America	1,947.5	1,935.8	−0.1
Western Europe	1,168.9	1,217.3	0.4
Japan	310.8	340.2	0.9
Australasia	63.9	89.5	3.4
Latin America	226.1	362.2	4.8
Middle East	78.7	125.7	4.8
Africa	96.0	181.3	6.6
South Asia	99.2	163.0	5.1
Southeast Asia	114.3	20.2	5.8
Soviet Union	836.5	1,242.0	4.0
Eastern Europe	353.9	455.4	2.6
China	334.9	522.1	4.5
World Total	5,630.7	6,834.7	2.0

Source: British Petroleum Co., *BP Statistical Review of World Energy 1982* (London: BP, 1983).

Table 1.2
World Crude Oil: Reserves and Production, 1983

	Reserves (billions of barrels)	Production (thousand barrels/day)
North America		
United States	29.8	8,669
Canada	7.0	1,396
Total	36.8	10,065
Latin America/Caribbean		
Mexico	48.3	2,702
Venezuela*	21.5	1,791
Argentina	2.6	481
Total	78.3	6,078
Western Europe		
Great Britain	13.9	2,260
Norway	6.8	600
Total	22.9	3,206
Asia/Pacific		
Indonesia*	9.6	1,292
Australia	1.6	405
India	3.4	390
Malaysia	3.3	370
Total	19.8	2,705
Africa		
Nigeria*	16.8	1,232
Libya*	21.5	1,020
Egypt	3.3	690
Algeria*	9.4	686
Total	57.8	4,548
Middle East		
Saudi Arabia*	162.4	5,071
Iran*	55.3	2,606
United Arab Emirates*	3.8	1,119
Kuwait*	64.2	1,111
Iraq*	41.0	905
Total	369.3	11,711
Communist Countries		
Soviet Union	63.0	12,388
China	19.5	2,107
Eastern Europe	2.6	450
Total	85.1	14,945
World Total	670.2	53,259

*OPEC member

Sources: Reserves: *International Petroleum Encyclopedia* (Tulsa, Okla.: Pennwell Publishing, 1983), pp. 293–95. Production: *Oil & Gas Journal*, December 26, 1983, pp. 80–81.

Table 1.3
World Natural Gas: Reserves and Production, 1983

	Reserves (quadrillion cu. ft.)	Production (trillion cu. ft.)
North America		
United States	204.0	17.7
Canada	97.0	2.5
Total	301.0	20.2
Latin America/Caribbean		
Mexico	75.8	1.3
Venezuela	54.1	0.6
Total	186.6	2.7
Western Europe		
Netherlands	51.9	2.1
Great Britain	25.4	1.3
Norway	58.0	0.8
West Germany	6.3	. 0.6
Total	156.7	5.7
Asia/Pacific		
Indonesia	29.6	0.7
Australia	17.8	0.5
Total	146.2	2.3
Africa		
Algeria	111.2	0.9
Other	78.2	0.3
Total	189.4	1.2
Middle East		
Saudi Arabia	117.0	0.5
Abu Dhabi	19.2	0.5
Iran	482.6	0.3
Total	769.7	1.7
Communist Countries		
Soviet Union	1240.0	17.7
Eastern Europe	29.8	1.8
China	14.0	0.4
Total	1283.8	19.9
World Total	3023.5	53.7

*OPEC member

Sources: Reserves: *International Petroleum Encyclopedia* (Tulsa, Okla.: Pennwell Publishing, 1983), pp. 292–93. Production: British Petroleum Co., *BP Statistical Review of World Energy 1982*, p. 8.

Table 1.4
World Coal: Reserves and Production

Country/Area	Reserves (billion tons)	1982 Production (million tons)
United States	219	697
Canada	4	36
Latin America	5	19
United Kingdon	49	121
West Germany	26	96
Other Western Europe	3	43
Soviet Union	160	558
Poland	29	189
Other Eastern Europe	3	39
China	109	618
India	13	130
Other Asia	3	82
Australia	29	94
South Africa	27	137
World Totals*	695	2,865

*Includes minor production from Africa, Middle East, and Oceania not elsewhere noted in table.

Sources: Reserves: U.S. Department of Energy, 1981 International Energy Annual (Washington, D.C.: U.S. Government Printing Office, 1982), p. 84; Production: BP Statistical Review of World Energy 1982, p. 10.

Table 2.1
Seven Majors' Control over Oil: Production and Buy-Back
(million b/d)

	1972	1982
Exxon	5.0	3.1
Royal Dutch/Shell	4.0	3.8
British Petroleum	4.8	2.4
Texaco	3.2	2.0
Standard of California	3.2	1.9
Mobil	1.9	1.7
Gulf	3.2	1.0
Total	25.3	15.9
World production*	41.3	38.5

*Excludes centrally planned economies

Sources: International Petroleum Encyclopedia, 1983; Petroleum Press Service, May 1972; Petroleum Economist, June 1983.

Table 2.2

The Biggest U.S. Oil Companies: 1983
(figures in billions of $)

Company	Fortune 500 rank	Sales	Profits	Assets	Employees (thousands)
Exxon	1	88.6	5.0	62.9	156
Mobil	3	54.6	1.5	35.1	178
Texaco	6	40.1	1.2	27.2	55
Standard Oil (Indiana)	8	27.6	1.9	25.8	57
Standard Oil (Cal.)	9	27.3	1.6	24.0	40
**Gulf Oil	11	26.6	1.0	20.9	43
Atlantic Richfield	12	25.1	1.5	23.3	50
**Shell (US)	13	19.7	1.6	22.2	35
Occidental	14	19.1	0.6	11.8	41
*U.S. Steel	15	16.9	(1.2)	19.3	99
Phillips	16	15.2	0.7	13.1	28
Sun	17	14.7	0.5	12.5	38
Tenneco	19	14.4	0.7	17.9	97
**Getty Oil	24	11.6	0.5	10.4	19
Standard Oil (Ohio)	25	11.6	1.5	16.4	44
Total		413.1	19.8	342:8	980
***Big Five		237.2	10.3	170.1	472

*U.S. Steel is classified as a petroleum company because of its acquisition of Marathon Oil Co.

**As of late 1984 these companies no longer exist as independent entities since they have been acquired as follows: Gulf Oil by Standard Oil of California (now named Chevron) and Getty Oil by Texaco; Shell Oil (U.S.) was in the process of becoming 100 percent owned by its parent, Royal Dutch/Shell, which in 1983 owned 69 percent.

***Exxon, Mobil, Texaco, Standard Oil (California), and Gulf.

Source: The Fortune 500, The 1984 Directory of U.S. Corporations (New York: Time Inc., 1984).

Table 2.3
Shifts in Oil Industry Ownership and Sales of Crude Oil and Products
(in percent)

	1970	1981
Crude Oil Ownership		
Big Seven	61	22
Other multinationals	33	19
Producing countries	—	59
State marketing companies	6	—
Product Sales		
Big Seven	50	40
Other Multinationals .	41	42
State enterprises	9	18

Sources: *International Petroleum Encyclopedia*, 1981, p. 426; 1983, p. 402.

Table 4.1
Crude Oil Production and Consumption in Western Europe
and Japan, 1982
(thousand barrels per day)

	Production	Consumption	Production as % of consumption
Western Europe			
France	33	2,070	1.6
West Germany	84	2,465	3.4
Italy	28	1,935	1.4
Netherlands	28	730	3.8
Norway	488	155	314.8
United Kingdom	2,050	1,555	131.8
Total	2,825	12,985	21.8
Japan	6	4,700	0.1

Source: *International Petroleum Encyclopedia*, 1983, pp. 322–24.

Notes

Introduction

page

9   Michael Tanzer, *The Energy Crisis: World Struggle for Power and Wealth* (New York: Monthly Review Press, 1974), p. 11.

9   Ibid., p. 12.

1. Fueling the International Economy

13   Data on comparative shares of different fuels in worldwide energy use are from British Petroleum Co., *BP Statistical Review of World Energy 1983* (London: British Petroleum Co., 1984), and David Crabbe and Richard McBride, eds., *The World Energy Book* (Cambridge, Mass.: MIT Press, 1979).

14   A good general discussion of the various historical stages in the development of the oil industry is provided in Harvey O'Connor, *The Empire of Oil* (New York: Monthly Review Press, 1955), pp. 8–18. The share of oil in U.S. energy consumption in the pre–World War II period is reported in American Petroleum Institute, *Petroleum Facts and Figures*, 1971 ed.

15   Data on the geographical distribution of energy consumption are reported in British Petroleum Co., *BP Statistical Review of World Energy 1983*, p. 32.

16   The effects of energy conservation are shown in "Energy Indicators," *OPEC Review* 7 (Winter 1983): 431.

16   For the proportions of energy supplied by domestic sources, see Michael Tanzer, *The Energy Crisis* (New York: Monthly Review Press, 1974), p. 16.

16   For information on domestic shares in energy supply as of 1983, see British Petroleum Co., *BP Statistical Review of World Energy 1983*, p. 13.

page

Data on oil reserves are from *Oil and Gas Journal*, December 27, 1982.

17   Production costs up to the early 1970s are discussed in M. A. Adelman, *The World Petroleum Market* (Baltimore: Johns Hopkins University Press, 1972), ch. 2. Recent cost figures are reported in *Oil and Gas Journal*, December 19, 1983.

17   The extent of the seven major companies' control of the oil industry up to 1950 is documented in U.S. Congress, Senate, Select Committee on Small Business, staff report to the Federal Trade Commission, *The International Petroleum Cartel* (Washington, D.C.: U.S. Government Printing Office, 1952), pp. 5–6, 23–25. For the shift in these companies' degree of control since 1973, see *International Petroleum Encyclopedia 1983* (Tulsa, Okla.: Pennwell Publishing, 1983), p. 402.

18   Walter Levy is quoted in Joyce Kolko and Gabriel Kolko, *The Limits of Power* (New York: Harper & Row, 1975), p. 447.

European Coal production figures are given in Crabbe and McBride, *The World Energy Book*, p. 237.

19   For U.S. oil import figures, see U.S. Department of Energy, *1981 International Energy Annual* (Washington, D.C.: U.S. Government Printing Office, 1982), p. 67.

19   OECD oil production and consumption figures are reported in *BP Statistical Review of World Energy 1983*, p. 5.

21   Data on changes in oil reserves are drawn from *BP Statistical Review of World Energy 1983*, p. 2; these are rough estimates, which we have indicated by showing an approximate range.

21   For the congressional study of oil resources, see U.S. Congress, Office of Technology Assessment, *World Petroleum Availability 1980–2000* (Washington, D.C.: U.S. Government Printing Office, 1980), p. 29. Coal and gas reserves are estimated in *1981 International Energy Annual*, pp. 82–85.

22   Per capita energy consumption is reported in *OPEC Review*, Winter 1983, p. 444.

25   For information on the early use of solar power, see L. Friedland, "The Power of Photovoltaics," *Sky*, November 1983.

25   Estimates of growth rates for photovoltaic installations are in *Photo-Voltaic Insider's Report*, April 1984, pp. 1, 6.

2. The Big Seven

26   Harvey O'Connor, *The Empire of Oil* (New York: Monthly Review Press, 1955), p. 10.

27   The brief history of the early years of the oil industry draws heavily on O'Connor, *The Empire of Oil*, pp. 10–18, and idem, *World Crisis in Oil* (New York: Monthly Review Press, 1962), chs. 1–7.

page
29   For details of the acquisition of concessions in the Middle East, see George Stocking, *Middle East Oil* (Nashville: Vanderbilt University Press, 1970), chs. 1–4.

29   For the majors' control of the industry in 1949, see U.S. Congress, Senate Select Committee on Small Business, *The International Petroleum Cartel*, (Washington, D.C.: U.S. Government Printing Office, 1952), pp. 24–25. For 1973, see *International Petroleum Encyclopedia 1981* (Tulsa, Okla.: Pennwell Publishing Co., 1981) U.S. Congress, Office of Technology Assessment, p. 421.

31   Data on reserves are in *World Petroleum Availability 1980–2000* (Washington, D.C.: U.S. Government Printing Office, 1980), pp. 14–20. The historical growth in importance of the Middle East as an oil-producing region is demonstrated in David Crabbe and Richard McBride, *The World Energy Book* (Cambridge, Mass.: MIT Press, 1979), p. 241.

31   Data on the importance of oil companies among the largest U.S. firms are from *Fortune*, May 30, 1984.

31   For the early history of vertical integration in the oil industry, see John McLean and Robert W. Haigh, *The Growth of Integrated Oil Companies* (Cambridge, Mass.: Harvard University Press, 1954).

32   Foreign production of the majors as of 1972 is in First National City Bank, *Energy Memo*, April 1974; for developments in the late 1970s, see *International Petroleum Encyclopedia 1981*, p. 426, and *Petroleum Economist*, June 1983.

33   The oil companies' move into petrochemicals is described in Jules Backman, *The Economics of the Chemical Industry* (Washington, D.C.: Manufacturing Chemists' Association, 1970), p. 73.

34   For the extent of oil company ownership of coal production, see U.S. Department of Energy, *Directory of Coal Production Ownership, 1979* (Washington, D.C.: U.S. Government Printing Office, 1981), pp. 7–29.

36   For the oil companies' strategy in solar energy, see *PhotoVoltaic Industry News*, March 1984, p. 4.

37   The quotation and the data on oil company acquisitions of mining companies are from *Big Oil's Move Into Mining* (Washington, D.C.: McGraw-Hill, 1983), pp. 70ff.

37   Data on copper mergers are from *Fortune*, April 30, 1984, p. 266.

3. Trade and the Flag

40   For a well-known expression of the view of multinationals as beyond shareholder and home government influence, see

page

Richard Barnet and Ronald Muller, *Global Reach* (New York: Simon & Schuster, 1974), especially chs. 4 and 10.

42   The quotation of Exxon's treasurer is from Robert Engler, *The Politics of Oil* (New York: Macmillan, 1961), p. 267, and the discussion of personnel interchange between the oil companies and government is from ibid., pp. 310–12.

43   The *Wall Street Journal* story is dated June 17, 1974, p. 28.

43   For the Sherrill quotation, see Robert Sherrill, *The Oil Follies of 1970–80: How the Petroleum Industry Stole the Show (and Much More Besides)* (Garden City, N.Y.: Anchor Press/Doubleday, 1983), p. 507.

44–50   The discussion of the role of the British and American governments in Middle East oil matters draws heavily on Harvey O'Connor, *World Crisis in Oil* (New York: Monthly Review Press, 1962), chs. 3, 23, and 25–27.

44–45   The discussion of Shell's early history and its view of competition as war is from O'Connor, *The Empire of Oil*, p. 30.

45   The quote from the British officer is in O'Connor, *World Crisis in Oil*, p. 279; the Churchill quotation is from ibid., p. 282.

46   The British government view is in O'Connor, *World Crisis in Oil*, p. 282; the U.S. Secretary of State's cable in ibid., p. 284; and the U.S. Ambassador's view in ibid., p. 287.

47   Exxon's president is quoted in O'Connor, *World Crisis in Oil*, p. 307; State Department and British Foreign Office statements are in ibid., p. 306.

49   King Saud's statement reported in "Report by Oil Companies of Effect of Anti-trust Suit in the Middle East, January 23, 1954," Hearings before the Subcommittee on Multinational Corporations of the Committee on Foreign Relations, U.S. Senate, Ninety-third Congress, Second Session [1974; "Church Committee Hearings"], on Multinational Petroleum Companies and Foreign Policy, Part 8, p. 29.

50   The State Department memo is quoted in Engler, *The Politics of Oil*, pp. 191–93.

51   For the details of the Mexican situation up to the nationalization of 1938, see L. Pazos, *Mitos y Realidades del Petroleo Mexicano* (Mexico: Editorial Diana, 1979), ch. 2.

51–52   The entry of U.S. oil companies into former European colonies is described in Victor Perlo, *American Imperialism* (New York: International Publishers, 1951), pp. 172–91, and Joyce Kolko and Gabriel Kolko, *The Limits of Power*, (New York: Harper & Row, 1975), p. 448.

52   The U.S. ambassador to Bolivia is quoted in Kolko and Kolko, *The Limits of Power*, pp. 416–17.

52   For data on the U.S. share of Middle East oil reserves in the

page

1940–50 period, see Zuhayr Mikdashi, *A Financial Analysis of Middle Eastern Oil Concessions 1901–1965* (New York: Praeger, 1966), p. 91.

53   A detailed discussion of the Iranian oil nationalization is in Michael Tanzer, *The Political Economy of International Oil and the Underdeveloped Countries* (Boston: Beacon Press, 1969), pp. 321–26.

53   The quotation is from David Wise and Thomas B. Ross, *The Invisible Government* (New York: Random House, 1964), p. 110.

53   Kim Roosevelt's subsequent move to Gulf is noted in Wise and Ross, *The Invisible Government*, p. 110.

54   The quotation is from Anthony Eden, *Full Circle* (Boston: Houghton Mifflin, 1960), p. 647.

54   The *New York Herald Tribune* report is quoted in David Horowitz, *The Free World Colossus* (New York: Hill & Wang, 1965), p. 191.

54–55   The *New York Times* report and the Engler comment are in Engler, *The Politics of Oil*. The Dulles statement is in C. Wright Mills, *The Causes of World War III* (New York: Simon & Schuster, 1958), p. 66.

55   For details of Kassem's overthrow, see Horowitz, *The Free World Colossus*, p. 192.

55   The Walter Levy quotation is from his article, "Oil Power," in *Foreign Affairs* (1974).

57–58   For a more complete discussion of the role of the World Bank in supporting overseas investment by multinational corporations, see Cheryl Payer, *The World Bank: A Critical Analysis* (New York: Monthly Review Press, 1982).

56–57   The OPIC quotation is from (unpublished) material presented by OPIC at a series of meetings for mining company executives in 1978.

58   The bank's role in deterring government participation in oil exploration and development is discussed in Tanzer, *The Political Economy of International Oil and the Underdeveloped Countries*, pp. 90–106. For a cautious examination of the bank's role in oil lending in the third world, see Michael Tanzer and Stephen Zorn, "The World Bank's Role in Petroleum Finance: A Critical Analysis," paper presented at the United Nations Meeting of Ad Hoc Group of Energy and Petroleum Experts on "Energy in the Eighties," New York, December 14–18, 1981.

58   The bank's post-1977 position in favor of oil lending is described in World Bank, *1978 Annual Report* (Washington, D.C.: The World Bank, 1978), pp. 20–22.

58–60   The bank's petroleum-related loans are described in World

page

Bank, *Petroleum Projects Press Releases FY 77–FY 82* and *Energy Projects Press Releases FY 83* (Washington, D.C.: World Bank, 1983).

4. Caught in the Squeeze

62–63   The French position in international oil is discussed in detail in Farid W. Saad, "France and Oil: A Contemporary Economic Study" (Ph.D. diss., Massachusetts Institute of Technology, 1969).

63   French oil interests in Algeria are discussed in *Petroleum Economist*, March 1974, pp. 88–89.

64–66   The discussion of the French role in Iraq is based on reports in the *New York Times*, May 16, 1967; the *Wall Street Journal*, February 15, 1974, p. 23; *Petroleum Intelligence Weekly*, October 23, 1967; *Oil and Gas Journal*, October 6, 1967, p. 69; and the *New York Times*, December 13, 1967.

65   The reference to De Gaulle is from *Oil and Gas Journal*, November 6, 1967, p. 69.

65   Buckley's talk was reported in the *New York Times*, December 13, 1967.

66–69   The discussion of Germany's pre–World War II oil policy draws heavily on Harvey O'Connor, *World Crisis in Oil* (New York: Monthly Review Press, 1962), pp. 49–52, 67–68, and 303–5.

69   For data on Deminex, see VEBA AG, *1983 Annual Report* (both VEBA and Deminex are partially owned by the West German government).

69–71   Italy's early petroleum history is described in detail in P. H. Frankel, *Mattei: Oil and Power Politics* (New York: Praeger, 1966), pp. 31–62.

70–71   The *Petroleum Intelligence Weekly* analysis of ENI's post-Mattei strategy is quoted from Michael Tanzer, *The Political Economy of International Oil and the Underdeveloped Countries*, (Boston: Beacon Press, 1969), p. 40.

71–73   For details on Japan's oil strategy, see Richard O'Connor, *The Oil Barons* (Boston: Little Brown, 1971), pp. 328–30; Robert Guillain, *The Japanese Challenge* (New York: Lippincott, 1970), p. 169; and J. E. Hartshorn, *Politics and World Oil Economics* (New York: Praeger, 1962), p. 287.

73   The increasing role of the Japanese government and national oil companies in Japan's crude oil supply is shown in *International Petroleum Encyclopedia 1982* (Tulsa, Okla.: Pennwell Publishing, 1982), p. 13.

74   Data on oil-import bills are from International Monetary Fund, *International Financial Statistics*, July 1982.

page

5. Rich But Not Powerful

76–77   For OPEC production figures, see *International Petroleum Encyclopedia 1983* (Tulsa, Okla.: Pennwell Publishing, 1983), pp. 320–24.

77–78   The quotation is from Harvey O'Connor, *World Crisis in Oil* (New York: Monthly Review Press, 1962), pp. 106–7.

78   The discussion of the Persian concession is from George Stocking, *Middle East Oil* (Kingsport, Tenn.: Vanderbilt University Press, 1965, pp. 5–6.

78–79   For Iraq, see ibid., p. 51.

79   The quotation from Socal is from Ed Shaffer, *The United States and the Control of World Oil* (London: Croon Helm, 1983), p. 66; see also Fred Halliday, *Arabia Without Sultans* (New York: Vintage Books, 1975), p. 62.
On Venezuela, see O'Connor, *World Crisis in Oil*, pp. 128–30.

79   Edwin Lieuwen is quoted in O'Connor, *World Crisis in Oil*, p. 135.

79–80   For the majors' share of crude oil production, see the discussion in Chapter 2.

79–80   Data on pre-1973 prices are in M. A. Adelman, *The World Petroleum Market* (Baltimore: Johns Hopkins University Press, 1972), ch. 6.

80   OPEC countries' oil revenues are reported in *Petroleum Economist*, June 1984, p. 217.

80   Adelman's price projections are in ibid., pp. 261–62.

82–83   On the stagnation of OPEC oil production, see Michael Renner, "Restructuring the World Energy Industry," *MERIP Reports*, January 1984, p. 15.

84–85   "Social indicators" for the Middle East countries can be found in World Bank, *World Development Report 1983* (Washington, D.C.: World Bank, 1983), pp. 186–97.

85   The quotation is from Joe Stork, "Ten Years After," *MERIP Reports*, January 1984, pp. 5–6.

85–86   The quotation is from P. Shaw, "The Political Economy of Inequality in the Arab World," *Arab Studies Quarterly*, Winter/Spring 1984, pp. 126–7.

86   The quotation is from G. Talhami, "The Inter-Arab Development Gap," *Arab Studies Quarterly*, Winter/Spring 1984, p. 162.

87   The quote is from Atif Kubursi, "The Arab Thrust into the international Arena: Pitfalls and Implications of Strategic Behavior," *Arab Studies Quarterly*, vol. 6, nos. 1 & 2 (1984).

88–91   The theoretical discussion of "Private Profits" and "Waste and Private Gain" is taken from Michael Tanzer, "Stealing Third World Resources." *Monthly Review*, April 1984, pp. 31–35.

page
89   The Sabic advertisement appeared in the *New York Times*, June 16, 1984.

91–92   The advertisement cited appeared in the *Wall Street Journal*, May 25, 1984, p. 18. (The quotations on pp. 5-20 and 5-22 are also from this advertising supplement and appeared at pp. 20 and 19 of the same issue of the *Wall Street Journal*.)

6. On the Margins

93   Oil consumption data are from *International Petroleum Encyclopedia 1983* (Tulsa, Okla: Pennwell Publishing, 1983), p. 325; data on exploration effort are from ibid., p. 319.

96   On the issue of "permanent sovereignty over natural resources," see Hasan Zakariya, "New Directions in the Search for and Development of Petroleum Resources of the Developing Countries," *Vanderbilt Journal of Transnational Law* 9 (1976): 545–77, and Stephen Zorn, "Permanent Sovereignty Over Natural Resources: Recent Developments in the Petroleum Sector," *Natural Resources Forum* 7 (October 1983): 321–28.

98–99   The reliance of developing countries on petroleum is documented in World Bank, *A Program to Accelerate Petroleum Production in the Developing Countries* (Washington, D.C.: World Bank, 1979), p. 3.

99   For the World Bank's pre-1977 views, see Walter J. Levy, Inc., "The Search for Oil in Developing Countries" (report to the World Bank, Nov. 1960).

103   The quotation is from P. H. Frankel, *Mattei* (New York: Praeger, 1966), p. 28.

104   For information on state oil companies, see U.N. Center for Natural Resources, Energy and Transport, *State Petroleum Enterprises in Developing Countries* (New York: Pergamon, 1980).

104–5   For data on the changing terms of petroleum agreements, see U.N. Center on Transnational Corporations, *Alternative Arrangements for Petroleum Development* (New York: United Nations, 1982), pp. 3–6.

7. Avoiding the Energy Crisis

106–7   The discussion of the early history of the Soviet oil industry relies heavily on Harvey O'Connor, *World Crisis in Oil* (New York: Monthly Review Press, 1962), pp. 29–36, 45, 61, 79–90 and 387.

107   For the current and projected future output of the Soviet oil industry, see *International Petroleum Encyclopedia 1983*

page

(Tulsa, Okla.: Penwell Publishing, 1983), pp. 214–25.

107   The historical figures on relative shares of various energy sources are from Robert W. Campbell, *The Economics of Soviet Oil and Gas* (Baltimore: Johns Hopkins University Press, 1968), pp. 1–15.

108   A more detailed description of the various phases of Soviet energy policy can be found in Michael Tanzer, *The Political Economy of International Oil and the Underdeveloped Countries* (Boston: Beacon Press, 1969), pp. 78–89.

109   The quotation is from National Petroleum Council, *Impact of Oil Exports from the Soviet Bloc* (Washington, D.C.: National Petroleum Council, 1962), p. 41.

110   The CIA report on Soviet oil is discussed in *Petroleum Economist*, June 1980, pp. 230–1. Soviet exports to Western Europe are described in U.S. Congress, Senate, Committee on Governmental Affairs, Hearings, *Soviet Energy Exports and Western European Energy Security* (Washington, D.C.: U.S. Government Printing Office, 1982).

111   For the early history of China and oil, see O'Connor, *World Crisis in Oil*, pp. 37, 60.

112–13   The post-1949 history of the Chinese oil industry is described in detail in "China's Oil and Energy Industries," *Petroleum Economist*, November 1981, pp. 476–98. This article also provides details on the oil companies' seeking exploration rights in China.

113   A recent review of oil company exploration in China is in *International Petroleum Encyclopedia 1983*, pp. 198–207.

113–72   Documentation for this discussion of the struggle over the role of oil in the Vietnam war, unless otherwise indicated, is drawn from the following: "Statement of Dr. Michael Tanzer, President, Tanzer Economic Associates, New York, N.Y.," in Hearings before the Committee on Foreign Relations, U.S. Senate, 92nd Congress, First Session, on S.1656 and S.1657," ("Foreign Assistance Legislation, Fiscal Year 1972"), June 10, 11, and 14, 1971, pp. 203–16. Appended to this statement are reprints of two valuable documents: Gabriel Kolko, "An Economic Incentive for Winning the War? Oiling the Escalator," *New Republic*, March 13, 1971, and "Vietnam and Oil—#1," a press digest and chronology prepared by the Peace Education Division of the American Friends Service Committee, Philadelphia, Pa., April 19, 1971.

114   Statement on the projected work pace for the Asian Pacific from *Petroleum Engineer*, June 1970, p. 51.

114   Quotation of State Department official from *Business Week*, October 24, 1970.

114   South Vietnam oil law information from *New York Times*, April 2, 1971.

page
114–15   On OPIC plans, see *Platt's Oilgram News Service,* March 10, 1971, p. 5, and *Village Voice,* March 25, 1971.

115   On Saigon plans for issuing leases, see *Journal of Commerce,* April 1, 1971.

115   "Are our sons dying for offshore oil?" was first raised by the California-based antiwar group Another Mother for Peace, in its February 1971 *Bulletin.*

115   On the role of progressive technical and political experts, see "Critics of U.S. Oil Policies in Vietnam Shift Focus of Their Attacks," *New York Times,* April 2, 1971, p. 2; on the letters sent to Congress, see statement by Senator Aiken, "The Indochina Oil Situation," *Congressional Record—Senate,* March 11, 1971, p. S 2911.

115   For *Oil and Gas Journal* "reversal," compare editorial in June 28, 1971, issue entitled "Leasing now off South Viet Nam would be major blunder" with its earlier "Fiction & Fact" article March 22, 1971, stating that "an unbelievable campaign blaming the American oil industry with working to prolong the war in Viet Nam has swept the country."

116   Speculation on role of speeded-up oil prospecting by S. Harrison, *China, Oil and Asia: Conflict Ahead?* (New York: Columbia University Press, 1977), p. 209.

117   The key elements of Vietnam's oil strategy are outlined in Michael Tanzer, "Oil Exploration Strategies for Developing Countries," *Natural Resources Forum* 2 (1978): 319–26.

120   *Wall Street Journal,* January 11, 1982, p. 31.

120   Report on Soviet-Vietnamese cooperation and claimed effect of U.S. technology embargo from *Petroleum News: Southeast Asia,* January 1981, pp. 59–60; reports of an initial Soviet find offshore Vietnam from *Oil and Gas Journal,* July 2, 1984, p. 43.

121   Observation of Western diplomat reported in *Far Eastern Economic Review,* April 28, 1983, p. 54.

121   Nguyen Hoa quoted in *Petroleum News: Southeast Asia,* January 1984, p. 92.

8. Conclusions

124   For a comparison of petroleum prices in real (discounted for inflation) and current-dollar terms, see World Bank, *Commodity Trade and Price Trends,* 1983–84 ed., p. 110.

124   For energy import data, see *BP Statistical Review of World Energy 1983* (London: British Petroleum Co., 1984), p. 13.

125–26   For oil company profit figures, see *International Petroleum Encyclopedia 1983* (Tulsa, Okla.: Pennwell Publishing, 1983), p. 402.

Index

159